Modern Political Development

Modern Political Development

Samuel H. Beer
Harvard University

Reprinted from *Patterns of Government*, Third Edition

Random House, New York

First Paperback Edition

987654321

Copyright © 1958, 1962, 1973, 1974 by Random House, Inc.

All rights reserved under International and Pan-American Copyright Conventions. No part of this book may be reproduced in any form or by any means, electronic or mechanical, including photocopying, without permission in writing from the publisher. All inquiries should be addressed to Random House, Inc., 201 East 50th Street, New York, N.Y. 10022. Published in the United States by Random House, Inc., and simultaneously in Canada by Random House of Canada Limited, Toronto.

Library of Congress Cataloging in Publication Data

Beer, Samuel Hutchison, 1911–
  Modern political development.

  "Originally published as Part 1 of the third edition of Patterns of government: the major political systems of Europe, edited by Samuel H. Beer and Adam B. Ulam . . . 1973."
  Bibliography: p.
  1. Constitutional history. 2. Comparative government. 3. Economic development. I. Beer, Samuel Hutchison, 1911– ed. Patterns of government. II. Title.
  JF31.B42   320.3   73-20358
  ISBN 0-394-31819-6

Manufactured in the United States of America

Foreword

This volume is a paperbound edition of Part 1 of the third edition of *Patterns of Government: The Major Political Systems of Europe*. The larger work includes sections on Britain, France, Germany, and Soviet Russia, as well as this Introduction on modern political development—all now available as separate paperbacks.

The five parts of *Patterns of Government* are integrated by the common theme of modernization. But each country account is also written so as to be suitable for study either separately or in conjunction with other countries not considered in *Patterns*. In the latter connection one attractive possibility would be a combination that would include the United States; for in each of the country accounts of *Patterns* a comparison with America, seen as a typical modern polity, is never far in the background of the analysis. Whatever one's preference, the present publication of the introduction and the country accounts as separate books provides the necessary flexibility.

A word about the general approach of *Patterns*: After a brief eclipse, history is making a strong comeback in political science, largely under such headings as "modernization" and "development." A period of neglect was healthy, since it obliged political scientists to decide what use they really wanted to make of history. They certainly had to get rid of that dreary chapter vaguely entitled "Historical Background" with which the textbook author used to preface his account of a country's government and politics and which constituted a sort of catchall of turning points, fundamental declarations, great statesmen, national characteristics, and bare and meaningless chronology.

In the third as in the previous editions of *Patterns*, a leading characteristic of the methodology is the use of both theory and history in the study of contemporary politics. The authors hold that patterns of political behavior in the present can be best explained if we have an understanding of how they originated and what traits they displayed in the past. In taking this view, the authors follow the example of some of the leading figures in modern political science, from Montesquieu to Weber, who used history to enlarge the body of empirical political theory and then used that theory to analyze and explain the historical process as it flows from the past through the present into the future.

Each country is examined as an example of a highly developed modern polity. This approach has two implications. First, it means emphasizing certain features the countries have in common. Second, it means treating these common features as the issue of a course of historical development moved by similar forces, passing through similar phases, and culminating in similar problems. But the stress on the common features of modernity does not lead the authors to overlook the crucial differences that distinguish the four systems. Quite the contrary. To show what is common helps them to bring out the differences more sharply. As a specialist in the country he is writing about, each author is accordingly concerned not only with its common modernity, but also with the traits and tensions that are unique to it.

In the country accounts the authors of *Patterns* have adapted this broad view of politics to their individual scholarly outlooks and to the material they deal with. In the Introduction I have set forth this approach in a more explicit and systematic manner. But I have not been concerned with theory alone. I have also gone on to apply theory to the development of the four countries with which *Patterns* is concerned. In doing so, I have, so far as possible, based my historical analysis upon the discussions of the individual countries.

The titles and authors of the paperbound editions of the country accounts are: *The British Political System,* by Samuel H. Beer; *The French Political System,* by Suzanne Berger; *The German Political System*, by Guido Goldman; and *The Russian Political System*, by Adam B. Ulam.

Harvard University   SAMUEL H. BEER

Contents

1	**Modernity and Its Disorders**	3
	The Loss of Purpose	4
	The Dominance of Technique	6
	The Response of Modernity	7
2	**A Model of the Political System**	9
	The Use and Abuse of Political Models	10
	The Means-End-Consequence Continuum	15
	The Problem of Political Order	18
	The Four Variables	22
3	**Political Culture**	24
	Origins of the Concept	25
	Belief Systems	27
	Systems of Value Orientation	29
	Systems of Expressive Symbolism	34
	Conceptions of Legitimacy	39
4	**Political Structure**	46
	The Pattern of Interests	47
	The Pattern of Power	50
	The Pattern of Policy	52
	Mobilization of Interests and Power	55
5	**The Dynamics of Modernization**	58
	History as Development	59
	Cultural Modernization	60

	Economic Modernization	66
	Political Modernization	73
	Approaches to Measurement	78
6	Elements of the Modern Polity	82
	Sovereignty and Bureaucracy	82
	Reformism and Secularism	86
	Nationalism and National Development	90
7	Stages of Political Modernization	94
	Development by Stages	94
	The Aristocratic Stage	98
	The Liberal Democratic Stage	102
	The Collectivist Stage	108
8	Problems of the Developed Modern Polity	112
	The Problem of Effectiveness	113
	The Problem of Authority	119

Statistical Appendixes

Appendix A	A Comparison of the United States, the United Kingdom, France, Germany, and the Soviet Union	128
Appendix B	Growth of the Electorates: Great Britain, France, and Germany, 1870–1970	132

Select Bibliography 133

Index 135

Modern Political Development

One

Modernity and Its Disorders

This book is about the modern political system, its development and its problems. Although I shall refer specifically only to four countries—Britain, France, Germany, and Russia—this distinctive political order flourishes in all advanced countries, bringing with it characteristic benefits and burdens. Moreover, most of the countries presently considered to be not advanced are also trying in their various ways to achieve a similar standing.

Thirty or forty years ago a book on this topic would have emphasized economic development and its consequences for government and politics. The interwar world brought to a climax the harsh problem of unemployment that had plagued industrial countries for generations. From this economic crisis new political fanaticisms arose that threatened to end not only the capitalist system of property relations, but also, in many countries, any hope for a democratic and liberal regime. As a result, political science in the thirties was obsessed with the prospect that a solution of the economic problem would bring to an end the old freedoms.

The concerns of government today still include the economy. Postwar governments have found inflation to be as intractable as prewar governments found deflation. These difficulties deserve to be examined in some detail, since they tell a great deal about the modern political system. Yet the problems that seemed to the prewar generation not only crushing but also insoluble have yielded to human control. Governments have demonstrated that they know how to achieve full employment and yet maintain democracy and freedom. When they have tolerated unemployment, as they have sometimes done in trying to restrain inflation, the magnitudes have been so slight as to have passed as indexes of prosperity in the thirties. Today the kind of issue that shakes the economic planning boards is how to increase the GNP by 5 rather than 2 percent per year. Viewed from the perspective of the Great Depression, this age of affluence would seem to have little to call a problem.

Yet if some of the problems today are less serious, others are more fundamental than those of the interwar years. They are more fundamental in the sense that they are rooted in the nature and structure of modernity itself. During the interwar period, it seemed to many students of politics that the advanced countries were confronted with a choice between a communist order in which the economic problem was solved but liberty was extinguished and a liberal order in which freedom was maintained but the economic problem could not be solved. The choice was sometimes put as "either liberty or groceries." Today it is readily seen that both sorts of regime, communist and liberal, are highly developed modern polities deeply disturbed by problems proceeding from their very modernity. These problems and disorders are visible in the Western democracies, including the United States. They also afflict Soviet Russia.

To identify the common problems of the modern polity is not to deny the major differences among the four systems being considered. On the contrary, from the viewpoint of human values as well as of system dynamics, the Russian dictatorship diverges from, and very probably will continue to diverge from, the three democracies. Seeing what they have in common only helps us see more sharply and understand more clearly their differences.

The Loss of Purpose

At the heart of the matter is the coincidence of loss of purpose with dominance of technique. Each has deep roots in the political culture of modernity and a long history of development in the modern period.

Loss of purpose here means not a loss of resolve or nerve, but rather a faltering or relaxation in people's sense of moral direction. This change is related to one of the great strengths of modernity, its liberating and democratic spirit. For modern government, the main legitimizing principle is democracy. Even modern dictatorships try to clothe coercion in the trappings of plebiscites and populistic propaganda. Yet democracy is a remarkably empty doctrine. It legitimizes what the people will, but it does nothing to give their will object and content.

The liberating thrust of modernity was a powerful weapon against the external coercions of monarchic and aristocratic rule and against the thought control of a monopolistic church, releasing vast energies and freeing more and more groups from the impositions of premodern regimes. Yet apart from such negations, the democratic doctrine holds up neither a vision for a people to pursue, nor an ideal by which an individual can mold his life. If the members of a nation—or a class or a group—do have a conception of common purpose, democracy will enable them to express it and to work for it. If they are trying to give themselves some such guide, democracy will provide them with the freedoms to seek it. But where positive goals are lacking, democracy itself will not supply them. People do ask for a purpose in life, seeking to find something greater than themselves with which to identify—a cause, a movement, a historical or moral reality. In this quest, the central legitimizing principle of modernity is at best neutral.

Without exaggeration, the criticism can be pushed harder. The modern spirit, it can be argued, is hostile not only to external but also to internal restraints. It is at war not only with the established authorities of earlier times, but also with the ethical systems inherited from them. It has been a major force in the attack on Puritanism, Victorianism, and traditional moralities generally.

We may well applaud these efforts as part of a necessary moral housecleaning in modern times and look forward to a "new" morality, better adapted to the needs of man and the age. This surely has been a recurrent mood in modern times. Yet by now experience must make us wonder whether any ideal of group or individual life can withstand the powerful negative thrusts of modernity. Any ethics, new or old, must impose restraints and direct behavior. In principle this immediately opens it up to attack as an illegitimate restraint upon deviant wishes. The repressions of the superego are no more to be tolerated than the oppressions of a ruling class. The liberating ethos of modern political culture is not merely neutral toward the problem of purpose but actively hostile to any solution.

These are, of course, only tendencies, not fully accomplished developments. Yet no one can fail to recognize the decline of purpose and the confusion and doubt over ideals that this decline entails in all advanced countries today. Its political consequences notoriously afflict the democracies and are central to the problem of legitimacy of government. But neither do dictatorship and authoritarian rule offer a ready and lasting solution. In Russia, Marxist-Leninist ideology did provide a firm moral basis for the Communist party and thus ultimately for the legitimacy and stability of the regime. But boredom and disgust with the spirit and tenets of that ideology grow constantly, confronting the rulers of party and state with their most critical challenge.

The Dominance of Technique

If the liberating spirit of democracy constitutes one of the moving forces of modernity, another and probably even more powerful force is science. At once an attitude, a method, and a body of specialized knowledge, science has increasingly influenced modernization. In recent years it has fathered a technological revolution that is transforming the world.

As an attitude the scientific approach—questioning, empirical, rationalist—has devastated the religious and philosophical conceptions on which the old political and personal moralities were founded. The long struggle between science and religion, in which religion has continually been forced back to an ever narrower range of influence in modern culture, is only one of the more familiar episodes. Nor has science, as attitude, method, or specialized body of knowledge, been able to supply the foundation for a new normative order. Quite properly not. The concern of scientific method, as of the various sciences, is with *how* something can be done, not with *why* it ought or ought not to be done. Being concerned with the means, science cannot answer questions relating to ends. In these ways, science has weakened the hold of old values without generating new ones. In relaxing a sense of moral direction, its effects have coincided with those of the democratic spirit.

When we think of the positive effects of science, we mean above all its technological consequences. From the earliest days of modern society, the application of new scientific knowledge to practical problems has been a major source of economic development. Increasingly, it has given the modern world the mastery over nature that the early philosophers of modernity passionately willed. Industrialization is the leading instance, a qualitative leap in the extension of human power over the environment that has no parallel in recorded history. Yet as the course of industrialism shows in its later as well as its earlier phases, this extension of human power has a tendency to create new problems as fast as it solves old ones. Thus the factory system raised human productivity to a new level, yet at the same time created the industrial city with its unprecedented and unanticipated social problems. As pollution in its many forms today gives evidence, an environment remade by man can be as hostile as pristine nature. The seemingly uncontrollable effects of technology afflict planned as well as unplanned economies, communist as well as capitalist states. Surely the most sobering instance of this distinctively modern disorder, a technology that has gotten out of control, is the development of nuclear weapons. We have learned that problem solving is a principal source of our problems.

The irony is that the instruments invented to facilitate the achievement of human goals lead to consequences their inventors never intended. It is the old story of industrial civilization, of the machine taking control. Modern technology does achieve remarkable results. At the same time, its unanticipated consequences for man and environment embody goals no one intended or even foresaw. Means dictate ends. Technique is dominant.

Politics illustrates an even more important facet of the problem. Public policy gets more and more complex and technical. In part this is because the problems of a developing society become more and more complicated. Yet we can also distinguish the heightening of complexity caused by the growth of knowledge itself. Government policies to deal with inflation, for instance, are complex because such factors as wages and prices are intricately interrelated with one another and with other economic factors. But these policies are also complex because the economists' knowledge is increasingly sophisticated. For both reasons modern government makes constantly greater demands on professional expertise, and the professional-bureaucratic complex grows in numbers, competence, and power.

But how can the policy output of this situation be understood by the public in a degree sufficient to enable it to exercise democratic control? In spite of a rapidly rising level of education among voters, the gap between their capacities and the realities of the world continuously widens. But insofar as public policy escapes from popular comprehension and control, the opportunity is opened up that this vast, growing power will be exploited by some body more competent, although a good deal smaller, than the democratic electorate. Such an elite may serve purposes that are selfish or benevolent, ideological or traditional. Inherent in the situation is the possibility that this elite may consist of the very professionals and bureaucrats called into existence by the various technologies.

In their bureaucratic role, their task is simply the exercise of their knowledge and skill; ends and goals presumably come from some other source. But as democratic control relaxes—or as authoritarian control relaxes—the bureaucrat is left to follow the momentum of his expertise, practicing his skill and extending its sway. Again and in a more serious sense, technique becomes dominant.

The Response of Modernity

Modernization theory helps the political scientist understand the political systems he confronts in the developed and developing countries of the contemporary world. It enables him to see common features in systems that are otherwise very different. It enables him to identify problems common to these regimes that might otherwise be neglected or blamed on passing and parochial causes. Since these problems are rooted in the nature of modernity, it follows that modernity must take the blame for them. Far-reaching as such criticism may be, however, it does not necessarily imply that modernity itself was a wrong turning and a mistake but only that the modern polity, like any other political order, has the vices of its virtues.

In developing a critique of political modernity, I am not going to rail against science, technology, and the rationalist spirit. I am too fond of their fruits, material and ideal, and too much the creature of that nourishment. Quite apart from my preferences, which are interesting only because they are widespread, the point is that these dynamic forces of modernity cannot be made to reverse themselves and somehow take us back to a premodern age. We may bitterly regret that science and technology have burdened the world with nuclear weapons. But even if all nuclear weapons were destroyed, the knowledge of how to make them would remain, thus leaving intact the fundamental menace. Some vast physical catastrophe, such as a nuclear war itself, could eliminate the menace of nuclear war by reducing mankind to a prescientific condition. Conceivably, a similar result could follow from the cultural catastrophe of the thoroughgoing Luddite revolution recommended by some of the romantic enemies of industrial civilization. Since not many of us can wish for eventualities such as these, we are left with less grandiose alternatives. We can become more sophisticated about the second-order consequences of specific branches of technology; we can try to plan the directions of growth of the sciences; and we can learn to be more sensitive to the needs of affectual life. This strategy is merely what a mature modern outlook itself advises. In this spirit I offer my critique of modernity as an organizing axis for an explanation of the political disorders of advanced societies today.

Before turning directly to the topic of modernity and modernization, I wish first to explore the nature of the polity. Chapter 2 will develop a model of the political system reduced to its essentials, concluding with a statement of the problem of order that inheres in the polity itself. Chapter 3 on political culture and Chapter 4 on political structure will elaborate this sketch of the basic model. After these considerations of what can be called political statics, I shall turn to problems of dynamics. The mechanisms, trends and stages of political modernization will be examined in Chapters 5, 6, and 7. The final chapter will return to the questions broadly posed in these introductory pages, showing in more detail how modernity gives rise to the distinctive disorders of the contemporary polity.

Two
A Model of the Political System

The field of political science, like politics itself, is a scene of controversy. Among scholars differences of opinion rooted in ideological conflict may be further exacerbated by professional pride, so that the contention among intellectuals often exceeds that among men who are actually competing for power. These disagreements extend to fundamental questions. They concern definitions, methodology, and results; how research should be carried on, what is meant by politics and government, and to what extent major hypotheses have been substantiated. In this respect political science shares the fortunes of the social sciences generally, which, in contrast with the natural sciences, are in greater or lesser degree marked by severe and widespread controversy.

These disagreements should not be concealed. Neither should they be exaggerated. Rational inquiry in the spirit of scientific method makes progress even with regard to the complex and volatile subject matter of political behavior. In the course of time, continuing inquiry discredits some views and strengthens support for others. While enjoying nothing that compares with the success of the natural sciences, political science does constitute a gradually accumulating body of knowledge.

The Use and Abuse of Political Models

These incontestable generalities about political science need to be kept in mind. They mean that there is no single definition or model of the political system that is generally accepted among political scientists. They mean that whatever approach we take to a piece of research will necessarily be a choice among various possible approaches. So far as writers can do so economically and relevantly, they should make clear the nature of this choice by indicating the premises, analytical and normative, from which they proceed. For they are bound to have in mind some sort of answers to basic questions such as: What is a political system? What are its principal elements or functions? What are the main forces that under appropriate conditions give rise to development or at least to change? If the writer will attempt an honest answer to these questions he will by no means guarantee himself immunity from criticism, but he should make it easier for the reader to know what he is driving at and may very well enhance his own understanding of his task.

The study of comparative politics raises these questions with special force. If we were trying to give an account of the political system of only a single country, we might well be content to employ the headings provided by conventional discourse. Superior studies of American national government have been made in terms of a conceptual framework no more sophisticated than a fourfold division of the main elements into "the party system," "the Congress," "the presidency," and "the civil service."

For comparing political systems, however, terms with a higher level of generality are needed. Thus several Western democracies could be compared with respect to "the electorate," "the party system," "the legislature," "the executive," and "the bureaucracy." While such a scheme might be suitable for countries in Western Europe, it could only distort the study of Soviet Russia. There is in Russia an organization that calls itself a party. But in contrast with the major role of parties in democratic countries, its function is to control public opinion rather than to reflect it. Similarly, the Supreme Soviet is called the legislature, but it would be a waste of time to give this body the kind of attention called for by the House of Commons or the French Assembly.

Difficulties of this kind force us to a still higher level of generality. Although many structures of the Russian political system are very different from those of Western democracies, certain basic functions of government are performed in all countries. In any political system, for instance, there must be some way in which the main goals of governmental action are determined. In a democratic country this policy-making function may be performed by means of an intricate interplay among electorate, party system, and legislature. In Russia, on the other hand, it centers in the upper organs of the Communist party. In this sense, similar functions are performed by radically different structures in Russia as compared with the democratic countries of the West.

In comparative politics, as in any kind of comparison, the identification of differences depends upon the presence of underlying similarities. Two things totally different in every respect could not be compared. Political systems can be compared because they have in common the characteristics that make them political systems.

A logical implication of these truisms would seem to be a search for the basic functions that characterize any political system. These would consist in functions performed by differing structures within the system as well as functions performed by the political system as a whole in relation to the society of which it was a part. The search for some such model of the political system has inspired the long history of political theory. It has produced a rich body of hypotheses, though hardly universal agreement.

The variety of models available to the aspiring student of politics can be illustrated by looking at three approaches offered by modern political theorists. It will be neither necessary nor convenient to develop fully their implications for political analysis. But I will stress their conceptions of the relation of the polity to the social and economic environment, a point of fundamental importance on which their authors differ radically.

Very early in modern times John Locke sketched the classical liberal model of the political system. A brief passage from his *Second Treatise of Government* (1690) will indicate its outlines:

> ... there and there only is political society where every one of the members hath quitted this natural power [to preserve his property—that is, his life, liberty and estate], resigned it up into the hands of the community in all cases that exclude him not from appealing for protection to the law established by it.

In this model the members of a political system are not divided into antagonistic classes but constitute a fundamentally harmonious community united by the common purpose of protecting private property. Power is exercised by "men authorised by the community," and the purpose of its exercise will be the severely limited one of protecting each man's life, liberty, and estate.

The perspective on politics expressed in this model directs research toward a particular kind of problem, raising certain questions and suggesting in reply certain hypotheses. Although the community is fundamentally harmonious, the relations between government and community remain problematical. Government may breach its trust and deviate from an impartial protection of the rights of the citizens. Yet in the Lockean model, such deviations do not result from conflicts deeply rooted in human nature or class structure. They may therefore be controlled by adaptations in the machinery of government.

A preoccupation of the political scientist starting from Lockean premises, therefore, is to investigate the mechanisms—such as the division of power, checks and balances, rotation in office, and frequent elections—by which governments may be kept faithful to their trust. The product of such concerns has not been insignificant. Witness the long line of practical governmental reform in American history running from *The Federalist* to the present day.

During the era of industrialization, the Marxists developed their socialist model. A key passage in Friedrich Engels' *Origin of the Family, Private Property and the State* (1884) reads:

> As the State arose out of the need to hold class antagonisms in check, but as it, at the same time, arose in the midst of the conflict of these classes, it is, as a rule, the State of the most powerful, economically dominant class, which by virtue thereof becomes also the dominant class politically and thus acquires a new means of holding down and exploiting the oppressed class.

The true believer will accept this statement as an article of faith. The political scientist uses it as an instrument to stimulate and facilitate research. Such research will have a distinctive direction. The relation of the economy to the polity becomes the crucial object of inquiry, with more particular questions focusing on the role of economic classes in policy making and the influence of economic development on political development. In the light of this model, political life itself will have little autonomy. Political change will be a "reflex" or "echo" of economic change, and the role of political and intellectual elites will reflect their economic class position in the mode of production.

In neither the Lockean nor the Marxist model is the political process itself an important source of change. In the Lockean view men are "naturally" rational and bring a real though limited morality to their dealings with one another, independently of any social or political conditioning. This value system, inherent in their humanity, constitutes an underlying consensus, making social harmony possible even though government performs severely limited functions. Those functions consist mainly in settling conflicts that have arisen outside the polity. Disequilibriums occur in the environment; government intervenes in an effort to reestablish balance. From the consequences of such "inputs" from the environment, governmental activity and political development result. The political process is essentially reactive, not autonomous. In the Marxist model, needless to say, the role of political life is even more restricted. The polity responds to conflict externally generated, that is, to the basic conflict of class that determines political development in the post-gentilic and precommunist stages of history. Its response, however, is already determined by the economic position of the owning class, which is also the ruling class. In this model the polity is not reactive, but merely reflexive.

A very different view of the relation of polity and society is set forth in the model of that other great modern, Jean Jacques Rousseau. Far from being merely reactive or reflexive, his polity is autonomous and creative. Its powerful role is indicated in these lines from the *Social Contract* (1762):

> The passage from the state of nature to the civil state produces a truly remarkable change in the individual. It substitutes justice for instinct in his behavior, and gives to his actions a moral basis which formerly was lacking. Only when the voice of duty replaces physical impulse and the cravings of appetite does man, who, till then, was concerned solely with himself, realize that he is under compulsion to obey quite different principles, and that he must now consult his reason and not merely respond to the promptings of desire.

The drift of Rousseau's argument is clear and striking: The state is the source of human values. It does not simply reflect a value system inherent in human nature or produced by the economy. On the contrary, it is from the polity that men acquire their sense of "justice" and a "moral basis" for their actions. The significance of this broad hypothesis for political analysis is sharpened as Rousseau continues, spelling out the effect of ongoing political life upon the individual:

> By dint of being exercised, his faculties will develop, his ideas take on a wider scope, his sentiments become ennobled, and his whole soul be so elevated, that, but for the fact that misuse of the new conditions still, at times, degrades him to a point below that from which he has emerged, he would unceasingly bless the day which freed him for ever from his ancient state, and turned him from a limited and stupid animal into an intelligent being and a Man.

The virtue of the Rousseauist approach is that it may induce the student of politics to take seriously the hypothesis that the polity itself is a source of social and individual purpose. In this view the source of political "output" is not merely a political reaction to economic or social "input," but forces generated within political life itself. Moreover, what the political process creates is not trivial. These purposes, arising out of political conflict and maturing through political development, engage the motivations of members at deep levels of psychic commitment and identification.

In this view the polity is not merely a reactive mechanism to social and economic conflict. On the contrary, its vision of justice and value may well be the cause of conflict. It is not merely a device for solving problems thrust upon it by the environment; rather its conception of purpose creates problems by setting goals that challenge the environment. It is certainly not simply a decision-making process; on the contrary, its most important process is the course of political development from which emerge the values and standards by which decisions are made. Acting as members of the polity, men have not only a wide autonomy, but they also use that autonomy for crucial tasks of individual and collective self-development.

The Necessity to Choose

These three models of the polity are still very much in use and in dispute among political scientists. They do not exhaust, but only illustrate, the variety that the student of politics has available to him. It is impossible not to have in mind some such model—or confusion of models—when one starts on a piece of research. To make use of such a theoretical device, however, does not mean that one must inevitably confirm the hypotheses implied by it. Objective scholarship is possible, though by no means easy, and the results of research have been known to force the modification and even abandonment of long-cherished models. Yet the act of initiating inquiry represented by the adoption of a model is, in effect, a choice that directs research in a certain direction and toward certain answers and thus diverts it from other directions and other types of answers.

The adoption of a model is a choice in two senses. In the first place, a model identifies what is causally important. It singles out certain elements of the political system as those on whose effects attention will be focused. In the second place, the adoption of a model consists in a choice among ethical concerns. Analytical interest centers on causal sequences, but unavoidably the analyst gives attention to the sequences that have a bearing on human welfare. Politics and government are studied because people are interested in their relation to mankind or, more likely, some part of mankind.

In this sense, then, political inquiry will not be "value free." Any model of causal sequences will involve effects. These effects will occupy some place, high or low, in some scheme of evaluation. To investigate these sequences, therefore, is to investigate what happens to some human values. Even if the subjective concern of the student is pure intellectual curiosity, the objective concerns of his inquiry involve values. Moreover, the fact that no student of politics really does investigate effects that in his scheme of values are completely trivial confirms the common-sense conclusion that subjectively as well as objectively political inquiry will not be free of ethical concerns. Rational inquiry does make progress. Yet the controversies that have swirled around the nature of politics and government will not be settled by a few seminar meetings or journal articles.

The sources of bias will be examined in the discussion of ideology in Chapter 3. They are acknowledged here partly as a warning, but especially to alert the reader to a challenge of the following pages. In those pages a model of the political system will be developed. I believe this model to be well suited for understanding the modern polity. Yet it is a choice among analytic possibilities and, moreover, a choice that will conflict on a fundamental level with some of the classic perspectives on politics that have flourished in the past and still flourish today. Given the inevitably controversial nature of political science, I regard that as a virtue.

The Means-End-Consequence Continuum

The fact that we are dealing with human action suggests a general and quite simple scheme. Two elements of any human act are the *end* being pursued and the *means* used to reach it. A third element is the *consequence*—the outcome of the whole process. This scheme applies to instrumental action by an individual. It can also be applied to action by a collectivity, such as a political system. The analogy is not total; it does not mean that groups have personalities or that the state is a person. Yet a political system is like a personality system in that both are action systems. In both, goals are set, means are used to pursue them, and results flow from the process. Thus the means-ends-consequences scheme provides a starting point for constructing a model of the political system.

John Dewey spent a lifetime examining this basic category of human action from every conceivable viewpoint—logical, ethical, esthetic, and social—and founded on it a complex and imposing philosophy.[1] In developing the implications of the idea, we can do no better than follow some of the main lines of his account.

The relation of means and consequence can be compared to the relation of cause and effect. Like causes, the means are antecedent conditions that lead to some change in a situation. In politics they are instrumentalities of power by which policies are implemented; in economics, productive capacities from which goods and services flow. Means and causes are alike in another respect: Causes do not merely give rise to effects, but also enter into them and become them, as in processes of physical transformation. Similarly, while means and consequences are analytically distinguishable, in the process of action the consequences arise from and are constituted by the means. Dewey wrote:

> Paints and skill in manipulative arrangement are means of a picture as end, because the picture is *their* assemblage and organization.... Flour, water, yeast are means of bread because they are ingredients of bread; while bread is a factor *in* life, not just *to* it. A good political constitution, honest police-system, and competent judiciary, are means of the prosperous life of the community because they are integrated portions of that life. Science is an instrumentality of and for art because it is the intelligent factor *in* art.... The connection of means-consequences is never one of bare succession in time, such that the element that is means is past and gone when the end is instituted. An active process is strung

---

[1] John Dewey (1859–1952) was a philosopher, exponent of pragmatism, and long-time professor at Columbia University. Among his principal works are *Experience and Nature* (1925, 1929), *Human Nature and Conduct* (1922), *The Public and Its Problems* (1927), and *Liberalism and Social Action* (1935).

out temporarily, but there is a deposit at each stage and point entering cumulatively and constitutively into the outcome. A genuine instrumentality *for* is always an organ *of* an end.[2]

Means become consequences, as causes become effects. Yet in human action this continuum depends on instrumentalities, physical and technical, that are guided at every stage by some end-in-view. Unlike causes in a purely natural setting, the means employed in human action include not only physical entities but also the technique that makes the objects productive of results. Indeed, such skill, knowledge, and technique convert these entities into instruments of action. Here is a primary difference from purely natural process—unless, of course, we can make the case for teleology and immanent ends in nature. In analyzing natural processes, we start from a paradigm with only two terms, cause and effect, but to analyze human action, in addition to means and consequence, we need a third term, the end or goal. Again, while the end-in-view is an analytically separable aspect of the means-end continuum, it is not physically or chronologically distinct. Dewey laid great stress on this fact: that "the difference between means and end is analytic, formal, not material and chronologic." He wrote:

> The end-in-view is a plan which is *contemporaneously* operative in selecting and arranging materials. The latter, brick, stone, wood and mortar, are means [of building a house] only as the end-in-view is actually incarnate in them, in forming them. Literally, they *are* the end in its present stage of realization. The end-in-view is present at each stage of the process; it is present as the *meaning* of the materials used and acts done; without its informing presence, the latter are in no sense "means"; they are merely extrinsic causal conditions.[3]

In Dewey's model of human action, means do not exist apart from ends. We can analytically isolate a pattern or set of means and consider its possibilities and capacities; but in the actual world of process, these means will be serving some ends. Thus in the world of politics, any system of power will be used for some end or purpose, and as in the paradigm of individual action, this purpose will give it meaning.

Conversely, the consequences of any sequence of action become elements in the starting point of new action. They modify the environment and so become part of the means that the actor may use in further action as, for instance, a program of redistribution may so modify the economic environment as to create a new set of political forces. Moreover, this environment, as the situational aspect of the continuum of action, affects

---

[2] Dewey, *Experience and Nature,* 2d ed. (New York, 1929), pp. 367–368.
[3] *Ibid.,* pp. 373–374.

any new end-in-view that emerges. Goals, ends, objectives are not something "mentalistic" that are conceived apart from the helps and hindrances to their achievement presented by the situation. The model has built into it an allowance for the effect of situational or structural factors on purposive behavior. One major example is the way consequences of one sequence help shape the purposes pursued in a new sequence of action. Continuing his homely figure of speech about house-building, Dewey wrote:

> The house itself, when building is complete, is "end" in no exclusive sense. It marks the conclusion of the organization of certain materials and events into effective means; but these materials and events still exist in causal interaction with other things. New consequences are foreseen; new purposes, ends-in-view, are entertained; they are embodied in the coördination of the thing built, now reduced to material, although significant material, along with other materials, and thus transmitted into means.[4]

Finally, the distinction between end and consequence directs attention to another fundamentally important difference between natural process and human action. In the former, causes always have their appropriate effects. But in action, the means adopted by actors do not always lead to the end the actors propose. There will be consequences, but they may not be those intended. What is more interesting, the results may include the intended consequences and yet also a complex of new conditions that were quite unanticipated and that work against the desired end. The contingency of human effort, whether individual or collective, (in contrast to the necessity of nature) cannot be neglected by the social scientist. But he must be particularly interested in that variety of failure which results when human action defeats itself. The irony of counterproductive effort is deeply rooted in the possibilities of human action.

> Man finds himself living in an aleatory world; his existence involves, to put it baldly, a gamble. The world is a scene of risk; it is uncertain, unstable, uncannily unstable. Its dangers are irregular, inconstant, not to be counted upon as to their times and seasons.
>
> . . . Everything that man achieves and possesses is got by actions that may involve him in other and obnoxious consequences in addition to those wanted and enjoyed. . . . While unknown consequences flowing from the past dog the present, the future is even more unknown and perilous; the present by that fact is ominous.[5]

---

[4] *Ibid.*

[5] *Ibid.*, pp. 41, 43.

The Problem of Political Order

The basic paradigm of action by an individual provides the starting point for constructing a model of the political system. For any polity will be an action system—a system of means directed to certain ends producing a flow of consequences. But the means-ends-consequence paradigm does not have a specifically political dimension. It emphasizes the action of an individual, while political relations must involve a number of people. Economists can use the life of Robinson Crusoe to illustrate the fundamentals of their science, but the political scientist lacks a focus for his special discipline until Friday appears. Yet simply to add a social dimension does not make the paradigm into a political model since other sets of human relationships also are social-action systems without being polities. The political involves a special kind of relationship among the members of the action system. One essential, as the example of Friday in the world of Robinson Crusoe suggests, is that someone is giving orders to someone else. The political involves command-obedience relations, or what some political scientists term "domination" or "imperative control."

So long as we are concerned with the action of only one individual, politics does not arise. But let means and ends, those two elements of any action system, be differentiated and thereby associated with different actors, and a command-obedience relationship—and problem—comes into existence. It is interesting to speculate on what a polity would look like if there were no such differentiation of roles. Those who determined the ends of governmental action would be identical with those who carried them out; governors and governed would be the same—a perfect democracy à la Rousseau. In modern representative democracies, on the other hand, the eye is immediately struck by the distinction between a highly organized governmental machine that issues orders and the mass of the population that carries them out. This is by no means the last word on the distribution of power, and in due course we shall consider the complications. It need only be noted here that in all historical polities the differentiation between those who govern and those who are governed is marked and fundamental.

In order to clarify and elaborate the distinction, it will be useful to use terms developed by Max Weber in his classic analysis of the phenomenon of "domination" (in German, *Herrschaft*). In a political system we can identify, on the one hand, a "chief" or "supreme authority" (*Herr*) and, on the other, an "administrative staff" (*Verwaltungstab*), whose action is "primarily oriented to the execution of the supreme authority's general policy and specific commands."[6] A principal value of Weber's analysis is

---

[6] Max Weber, *The Theory of Social and Economic Organization,* A. M. Henderson and Talcott Parsons (trs.) (New York, 1947), p. 324. Weber (1864–1920), a German sociologist

that it identifies the basic political relationship as being between the element that determines the ends for which the power of the polity will be used and the element that constitutes the power to carry out those ends. In this way it shows the identity of the two basic processes of the political system with the two basic processes of the action system. The decision making of the chief determines the ends; the decision executing of the staff constitutes the means. The essential function of the "chief" in the Weberian model is the determination of ends, while the essential function of the "administrative staff" is the implementation of these ends. Thus is framed the primordial political problem of maintaining cohesion between the two basic elements of the polity, those who give commands and those who carry them out.

To focus on the relationship between the chief and the administrative staff passes over the question of how these two elements may be able as an integrated whole to control a still larger body. This is convenient for analysis, since it sets aside for the moment the possibility that this latter kind of control might be based solely on nonlegitimate means, such as force or manipulation, and concentrates on the essential question of how —and how far—chief and staff are cohesive and on the role of conceptions of legitimacy in maintaining this cohesion. The basic hypothesis is that such a conception of legitimate authority shared by chief and staff is indispensable to their cohesion.

This model of the polity, it must be emphasized, is not an account of the origin of the state. Its validity does not depend upon there ever having been an historical polity composed of a man who was a "chief" and a group constituting his "administrative staff." At the same time, the imagery it suggests, bringing to mind the simpler polities of tribal or feudal society, gives substance to the distinction being drawn. We think, perhaps, of the Indian chief who with regard to the means of hunting buffalo or fighting enemies is helpless in comparison with the assembled might of his braves and warriors, yet who by his authority is able to wield their power. Similarly, in the modern democratic polity, the power—in the sense of "power to," that is, the instrumentalities of physical strength, money, technology, property, and so forth—rests largely with the people, the governed. But they use this power in obedience to the commands of government in a crucial degree because they hold these commands to be legitimate. Similarly, within the governmental machine itself, the bureaucrats, who are in possession of the essential skills and tools of governmental action, carry out the orders of law makers and chief executives because these orders are believed to be legitimate. We sometimes think of those who issue the

---

and political economist, developed his analysis of the role of conceptions of legitimacy especially in a section entitled "Types of Authority and Imperative Coordination" in the volume translated by Henderson and Parsons.

orders as being those who have the power. But this conceals the *essential political problem, which is precisely and paradoxically why those with the means of power obey those who have only authority.*

The polity is an action system that enables a number of people to decide on ends and to pursue them. This statement has no necessary implication of democracy. It can equally well apply to a system in which one "chief" determines the ends. What the statement does mean is that however many take part in deciding on ends, all members basically accept the decisions. Thus what was otherwise a number of people incapable of acting purposively as a unit now acquires that capacity.

To acquire this capacity of unified purposive action is to acquire a political order. The political order is the system the members see and intend, the legitimate system of government. Yet in this political order, within various structures and between structures, those who govern and those who are governed will be differentiated. Governors and governed are potentially, though not inevitably, in conflict. Any political order contains within itself a major source of disorder.

Politics and Class

This analysis of political order and disorder can be contested. The principal source of conflict could be found outside the polity itself, as when it is argued that the economy produces a conflict of classes, which in turn is reflected in the polity. By contrast, I am arguing for the autonomy of the political. I would, for instance, question whether any economic class can act as a cohesive unit unless it has some kind of political system. Moreover, I would hypothesize that once such a system is established to govern the class, it may well be disrupted by the essentially political conflict of governors and governed—a hypothesis richly substantiated by the history of organizations based on economic class.

The model does tell us something about class and class conflict. But the classes it identifies, being based on the differentiation of governor and governed, are essentially political, not economic or social. To use Weber's terms, the "administrative staff" is the elementary form of the governing class. Between it and the other members of the system there exists a command-obedience relationship from which arises a problem of political order. This governing class may also acquire privileges in the form of private property, and considering its political power, it is almost certain to do so. Yet its basis and social function are political, and the flow of causation is from its activity as governing class to other functions. Thus, even if economic differentiations resulting from private property were removed, a governing class might very well persist. This model, in short, makes the persistence of a governing class in Soviet Russia, in the form of the Communist party, not a problem, but a natural occurrence readily assimilated to the basic concepts of our analysis.

At the same time, this approach with its stress on the political prevents us from taking for granted the capacity of any group for unified purposive action. It means we will doubt that economic class solidarity, however helpful, can remove the necessity for a political system. Moreover, its formulation of the basic political problem means that the governing class itself must be governed. Thus in Russia today, the problem of political order arises not only with regard to the authority of the Communist party in relation to the wider population, but even more acutely with regard to the relations of the party leaders and the rank and file. In a system in which terror and physical violence have played so large a role, especially under the dictatorship of Stalin, these relationships present with special vividness the vital importance of legitimacy in creating authority that can control power.

The model does not imply that conflict is inevitable in political systems. It does, however, point to the continuing possibility of conflict at whatever level there is differentiation between the two basic functions of any action system. Conceptions of legitimacy, supported by other forces, may effectively integrate the system. The political problem may be solved. The order may survive and flourish. Yet the model does not let us forget that quite apart from the projection into the polity of conflicts from nonpolitical sources—economic, religious, ethnic, and so on—the political order itself is problematical, containing within itself the possibility of disorder. Nor is disorder always bad, for conflict can be a principal motor of political development.

Politics and Vision

Theories of government often start from the premise that conflict among men arises from essentially nonpolitical causes—economic, psychological, ideological—and then go on to show how government is a response to this state of conflict, its function being perhaps to reconcile conflicts, suppress them, or exert force on behalf of one of the parties. In these models the extrapolitical situation determines the basic function of government.

But this merely responsive model of the polity underestimates the human imagination. Men use the polity for a far wider spectrum of purposes. Individual action shows a great variety of patterns to which men may commit themselves singly. The same is true of collective action by means of the polity. In our model we also begin from the fact that human behavior is purposive: hence the great stress on the means-ends-consequence continuum. This formula represents a fundamental category of human action that in its political form has given rise to an enormous variety of patterns of government. Like the individual, the polity is not responsive, but creative. The polity can as autonomously as the individual generate complex patterns of purposive activity. Using the word in a sense that is not utopian or sentimental, I will say that a polity, like an individual human being, will have its "vision." Political vision and political imagination are not mere incidents and ornaments of the political process, but fundamental and continuous forces in any political system.

At the same time that purposive action is undertaken by means of a polity, however, the possibility of conflict is brought into existence by the polity itself. The differentiation of ends and means in the form of governors and governed can hardly be avoided in any except perhaps the smallest and simplest societies. Yet this distinction creates the structural conditions for conflict. In this sense the political order itself is the source of one of its major disorders.

The Four Variables

The terms *means, ends, consequences,* and *legitimacy* suggest the principal elements of the model and their basic relationships. But we also need some terms that are closer to conventional usage in political analysis.

The term *pattern of interests* will be used to refer both to the process by which ends-in-view are determined and to those ends themselves. (1) As process, the pattern of interests consists of the fundamental business of policy making and goal setting in the polity. (2) We can also abstract from this process the ends-in-view or intentions entertained by the various groups and bodies taking part in it. "Interests" seems the best term to catch the general meaning, which, of course, is not confined to self-interest, material interest, or short-run interest, but includes all sorts of ends-in-view. In addition to the term pattern of interests, such terms as *pattern of policy making* and *pattern of basic decision making* will be used as synonymous, when the context makes them appropriate.

The term *pattern of power* also has a dual meaning. (1) Looked at statically, it means those instrumentalities, material and nonmaterial, that are available for carrying out the ends-in-view embodied in decisions on policy. These are the instrumentalities of power of the polity. The bureaucracy, military and civilian, is a leading element, but the pattern of power of the modern polity also includes organized groups in the private sector and even the ordinary citizen and his resources, insofar as they can be mobilized in the service of government decisions. (2) In its second meaning, the pattern of power refers to these facilities as they actually operate in the political and governmental process—for instance, the army fighting wars or the civil service implementing a program of conservation or welfare.

The *pattern of policy* is the output of the system. It is distinguished from the pattern of power as consequence is distinguished from means. The output of government consists of the specific powers of government in the process of being exercised. When we look at this process as policy and output, however, we are thinking of its relation to a further environment, such as the effect of a redistributive welfare program upon the society.

Finally, the *pattern of political culture* refers especially (but not only) to those orientations toward action which are called conceptions of legitimacy. Distinguishing this element of the political system is indispensable if we are to isolate and examine the crucial grounds of political order by which the pattern of power and the pattern of interests may be integrated.

Three
Political Culture

Analytically the problem of political order is to explain why some men give orders and others obey. This problem can be presented in a fairly simple stimulus-response model. The command is the stimulus and the response is the required action. We observe the chief giving a certain command to his braves and the action they sequentially and repeatedly take. In a sense we can observe the orders going out from the Internal Revenue Service and the response of millions of citizens as they pay their income taxes. These two sets of actions, stimuli and responses, are all that we can observe; it would be an immense relief if we could confine our attention to them and not have to concern ourselves with such unobservable entities as the "thoughts," "purposes," or "feelings" of the subjects being studied.

Such a confined investigation would indeed be the procedure of a strict behaviorism. That approach has been adequate to studying physical reflexes and to developing certain important laws of the association of input and output events in relation to human and other organisms. A strict behaviorism, however, has never made much headway in political science (or indeed in any other social science) because it cannot provide the complex framework necessary to explain most phenomena of peculiarly human significance.[1] In order to study these phenomena, we must suppose

---

[1] A psychologist, Charles E. Osgood, discusses this problem in his "Behavior Theory and the Social Sciences," in Roland Young (ed.), *Approaches to the Study of Politics* (Evanston, Ill., 1958).

between stimulus and response a set of intervening variables of great complexity. The variables include that whole world of motivation, conscious and unconscious, personal and cultural, which at an earlier date some philosophers of social science thought they had banished as "spooks" and "soul stuff."[2] Today political scientists are careful to call themselves not behaviorists, but behavioralists. And indeed the innovations in method and theory associated with the latter term give even greater emphasis to the subjective and psychological aspects of political action than did the traditional American approach to the study of politics. Broadly speaking, the function of the term "political culture" is to make sure that political analysis will give this aspect of political action the serious and systematic attention it warrants.

Origins of the Concept

In the long perspective of political inquiry, it is no innovation to stress such factors. The classic studies of political behavior—such as those of Montesquieu, Alexis de Tocqueville, Walter Bagehot, and James Bryce—have recognized the powerful role of ideas. One may cite Tocqueville's famous chapter in *Democracy in America* (1835–1840) on the "Principal causes which tend to maintain the democratic republic in the United States," in which he attributed the main influence to "manners," that is, "the moral and intellectual characteristics" of Americans. The question of method—the role of ideas and values and how they are to be studied—was sharply focused in the furious debates conducted mainly by German philosophers during the latter part of the nineteenth century. Taking this *Methodenstreit* as his point of departure, Max Weber, who by no means neglected the importance of structural forces, developed a sensible approach that, moreover, could actually be used in research, as he showed in his brilliant studies of the role of conceptions of legitimacy in political systems.

In American social science, the leading figure in importing and developing Weber's viewpoint has been Talcott Parsons.[3] His action frame of reference is based on the premise that human behavior cannot be explained unless the observer grasps its meaning to the persons interacting. Such meanings are shared among members of a system by means of a common culture. A culture is an "ordered system of symbols"—of which words are the most familiar, but by no means the only example—that

---

[2]The pejorative expressions are from Arthur F. Bentley's classic, *The Process of Government* (Chicago, 1908).

[3]Among the works of Talcott Parsons, a professor of sociology at Harvard, are *The Structure of Social Action* (1937), *Essays in Sociological Theory*, rev. ed. (1954), and *The Social System* (1951).

enables members of a system to see and sense in quite similar ways the situation, physical and social, in which they find themselves. In a social system, he writes, the members' relation to their situation is "defined and mediated in terms of a system of culturally structured and shared symbols."[4] It was a natural next step for the concept of culture to be applied to the subculture of that particular subsystem called the polity.[5] Thus the concept of political culture has provided a way of systematically thinking about and analyzing the "ordered systems of symbols" that play a crucial role in giving substance to the actions and interactions of human beings.

The political culture of a people gives them an orientation toward their polity and its processes. To be oriented is to have a sense of direction—in the simplest meaning, to know where you are in relation to the points of the compass. To be politically oriented would mean, in general, knowing how your government operates—having a "cognitive map" of the polity—and also knowing how it ought to operate and what it ought and ought not do—having a "normative map." Insofar as a people share such a cognitive and normative map, they will usually be able to act together, understanding what each is doing and avoiding conflict and dissension. "Usually" is the most we should say in this respect, since a political culture can have the effect of creating distrust and promoting dissension. Even then, however, it is performing the function of orientation—to a malevolent and unreliable world—giving members a sense of what is happening and what they can and ought to do. Insofar as a political culture is shared by the individual—that is, internalized in his personality system—it constitutes that very complicated intervening variable between the stimuli of the political situation and the responses of the political actor.

Culture exists because of the capacity for symbolic behavior that is especially, if not exclusively, characteristic of human beings. Symbolic behavior makes it possible for people to communicate, and so to learn from one another and to accumulate and pass on what they have learned from one generation to another. Language is the leading example of symbolic behavior. Through it we are able to communicate meanings—the ideas, values, and emotions that give life significance. Indeed, a great deal of social interaction consists in little more than the communication of such meanings. As anyone who has ever been to a cocktail party knows, social interaction can go on at a furious pace, crushing egos, creating and dissolving liaisons, and leading to triumphs and failures of factional purpose without anyone's moving more than a few feet from the spot in which he was originally standing.

As this example may suggest, language, while the leading kind of sym-

---

[4]Parsons, *The Social System* (Glencoe, Ill., 1951), p. 6.
[5]See especially Gabriel Almond, "Comparative Political Systems," *Journal of Politics,* 18 (1956).

bolic behavior, may be the lesser part. Tones of voice, body movements, who walks up to whom, and who is walked up to can communicate far more than mere words. In a school room, for instance, as much teaching is accomplished by what the teacher does as by what he says. The class is an action system with the instrumental purpose of getting certain bits of knowledge into the heads of children. At the same time, and also consciously and intentionally, it is designed to inculcate certain norms of conduct by the example of how the class is conducted.

Political life itself is especially rich in such symbolic behavior. The purely ceremonial occasions and institutions are well-known: Bastille Day in France, the Fourth of July in the United States, May Day in Moscow, the opening of Parliament in London. But the mixtures of instrumental and symbolic behavior are even more important. The national convention of an American political party is, instrumentally, a means of selecting a presidential candidate and drawing up a platform. But its symbolic aspect—while not perfectly understood or entirely intended—gives it a major teaching function. Only in this light can we make sense of its practices, which are highly dysfunctional when measured against the instrumental purpose: For instance, the number of delegates and alternates is huge, unwieldy, and unnecessary, but symbolizes populistic values. Thus while serving to select candidates and write platforms, the political convention has also been for generations a school that propagates American political culture.

Belief Systems

A moment of introspection will assure any political scientist that the world of political culture, as an operative element of the personality system, tends to be disorderly, ambivalent, and confused. If the concept is to be used in analysis, however, we must try to identify its main elements and to establish schemes of classification, even though such efforts must inevitably exaggerate the formality of the subject matter. I will follow here a division suggested by Parsons' classification of cultural-pattern types into belief systems, systems of value orientation and systems of expressive symbols.[6]

A political belief system is the "cognitive map" of a political culture; its function is to "define the situation." On the one hand, there is an objective reality, which the individual cannot change merely by his thinking and feeling, which he will incorrectly perceive at his peril, and to which he must adapt at least to the extent of using the right tools to control it. This is the situational or structural aspect of social action. But perception of the

---

[6]Parsons, *The Social System*, p. 327.

social, as of the natural, environment does not begin from a tabula rasa. The individual brings to his perception of the political situation a more or less coherent body of existential propositions about politics and government. Such ideas may extend to general orientations toward the political capacities and tendencies of mankind—for instance, optimistic folklore that "you can trust the people" and pessimistic folklore that "you can't change human nature." At a less general level, a political belief system will state what a particular political system is and how it operates. Survey research in the Western democracies does not encourage us to think that for most people this knowledge extends to details of constitutional principles or governmental machinery. Yet we should not underestimate the definiteness—and in many cases, the sophistication—of the ideas of the ordinary voter.

A function of an individual's political belief system is to help him perceive and interpret political events in his environment. Political events, however, are not mere physical realities. What the individual perceives in a political situation is not only the physical behavior of other individuals and groups—leaders, parties, legislatures, and so on—but also and especially the *meaning* of their physical behavior—a large part of which physical behavior is itself purely symbolic, for example, talking. The sheer physical behavior of the principals in a portentous Cabinet crisis, for instance, may be far less complicated than that involved in a game of sandlot baseball. The facts that the memoirists will reveal are such things as the heightening emotional tension on the part of the Prime Minister and his faction, the bluffing by his opponent, the coolness of some, the panic of others, the moral failure of still others, and the clever tactics and stupid blunders that led to the final breakup. A political situation consists of such subjective and psychological factors and forces as well as the overt, physical behavior with which they are associated.

Political culture is at once the source of the meanings with which men invest their behavior and the instrument by which those sharing a common political culture perceive and understand those meanings. A slight movement and a few words are understood by the man originating them and by the man to whom they are directed as a sincere gesture of friendship because both have the same cultural background. We can say that political culture coordinates political action, provided it is remembered that this can mean ordering not only harmonious action but also severe conflict, as when only a common subculture made the refined insults of the *code duello* intelligible and effective. Communication is a necessary foundation of political conflict. As Henry VIII remarked of the king of France, "Francis and I understand one another very well. We both want Calais." In the absence of some elements of common culture, there is no communication and so no political, or indeed human, conflict, but only the blind clash of physical forces.

If a common political culture performs such a function for members of a political system, it is evident why the political scientist must gain access to the same cultural background if he is to understand and explain their behavior. Such understanding, it must be emphasized, is just as necessary for structural as for cultural analysis. A political situation may exercise powerful compulsions on the people in it, and analysis of the regularities that may be set up by such structural forces is one of the most important and exciting kinds of political analysis. Yet a political situation, as we have seen, is not to be understood apart from the meaningful action of its participants. The very compulsions that it exercises upon them depend in large part upon the meanings they find in the situation. If we are to understand these compulsions, we must understand the meaning given the situation by the common culture of the participants.

A stimulus-response model for political analysis is not useless. Even if the analyst has only a limited knowledge of a political culture, he may find situations that are similar in terms of those limited categories. He can isolate such situations, compare them, and conceivably find similar consequences flowing from them. Such a correlation is not to be disdained. Yet there is always the chance that it has overlooked crucial explanatory and causal factors. There may be important similarities that would have been revealed by a better understanding of the purposes, style, and operative ideals of the people being studied. If so, the situations will have been incorrectly identified and compared, and the correlation will have no predictive power.

Or again, actions that are superficially similar may be very different in terms of the different cultures involved. For instance, attending church by Protestants or Catholics has an entirely different significance from going to the mosque for Moslems. In such a case, what seems to be the discovery of a uniformity—the correlation of attending church or mosque with some sort of other behavior—may be false and misleading. The chance of such error, substantial enough when one is comparing systems within the same general cultural region, such as Europe, is even greater when countries in different cultural regions are being compared. The attempts by some social scientists to approximate the modernizing process in developing countries today with that in Europe in recent centuries abundantly illustrate the dangers.

Systems of Value Orientation

Values are standards of selection among alternatives of action.[7] Even the most tightly compelling situation leaves open some choice to the individual

---
[7] *Ibid.*, p. 12.

confronting it, although it may be only the choice between sink or swim. Some acts of choice may be purely reflexive or instinctual, and some may be totally determined by unconscious motivation. A basic hypothesis of the action frame of reference, however, is that standards defining what is desirable and worthwhile play an important role. The response of the individual to a situation will depend not only upon the "cognitive map," but also upon the "normative map" that he brings to the perception of the situation.

Values may be classified as cognitive, appreciative, and moral. Cognitive values include such standards as the rules of logic or scientific inquiry. These are norms setting out correct methods of thinking and conducting research. Appreciative values are conceptions of what is worthwhile for an individual to have or be. They include definitions of success or excellence, such as the classical standards of *arete* or Renaissance notions of *virtù*, and, as these references suggest, vary from one culture to another. They range from the high valuation of military prowess and monastic austerity in the medieval world through the reversal of values by modernity, which gives an equally high place to secular success in money making and bureaucratic problem solving.

Moral values, which constitute the third class, are standards of choice defining rights and duties between individuals and groups. Typically, they lay down rights and duties in such relationships as those between parent and child, husband and wife, old and young, and buyer and seller and regulate conduct in sexual, family, economic, and other social spheres. Political values are a subclass of moral values regulating command-obedience relationships and other questions of what is right and good for the collectivity. Among political values, it is important to distinguish between conceptions of authority and conceptions of purpose.

Any scheme of classification will exaggerate the sharpness and formality of such cultural elements as they actually function in personality and action systems. The distinction between belief systems and value systems itself may need at times to be severely qualified. Looked at from the viewpoint of modern philosophy, the difference between existential and normative propositions—between statements of what "is" and what "ought to be" —seems fundamental and indeed unbridgeable. Looking at the matter historically, however, we readily see that in some cultural systems the distinction between "is" and "ought" has not been drawn with such sharpness. In classical thought, for instance, with its stress on teleology and an objective moral order, the difference between what actually happens and what ethically ought to happen was not marked. In importing into my classification of cultural patterns a distinction between belief systems and value systems, I may be succumbing to a cultural outlook that is peculiarly and parochially modern. For, as we shall see, the modern stress on subjectivity in the realm of values logically leads to a rigid separation of this realm from the world of objective reality.

While typical modern philosophies insist on a sharp separation between fact and value, in actual practice modern political culture is less than faithful to this standard. As the great "isms" of the contemporary world demonstrate, modern political man—however illogically—does continually leap back and forth between fact and value in constructing and using the "maps" by which he tries to understand and control political situations. To such maps, which are at once cognitive and normative, it is useful to apply the term "ideology." In this sense Marxism-Leninism is an ideology. On the one hand, it purports to be an objective, indeed scientific, description and explanation of the development of world history. Specifically, it lays down as a matter of fact that Russian society will be led through the present stage of socialism by the Communist party, acting as the vanguard of the proletariat. Strictly understood this system of belief does not state what "ought" to happen or what anyone "ought" to do. Yet no reader can miss the tone of moral exhortation in which these descriptions and predictions are uttered. Nor would any political scientist fail to observe that Marxist-Leninist ideology embraces political values that endow the Communist party leaders with authority and their policies with the ethical sanction of common purpose.

The systems of thought that men follow in actual political behavior are prone to be ideological. In plain words this means that the propositions political actors offer as nothing but the unvarnished truth are in fact heavily laden with their value preferences. To demonstrate this we need not turn to some Germanic *Weltanschauung*. Ask anyone what he thinks are the causes of crime, poverty, political corruption, war, economic productivity, or any other such topic of current interest and you almost certainly will get an answer bringing with it a strong whiff of ideology. Nor can the political scientist or social scientist be snobbish about the matter. He is likely to catch the ideological scent in the writings of his colleagues as well as in the talk of the man in the street.

Sources of Bias

The sources of ideological bias may be psychological. One of the uses of the concept of political culture is that it makes it easier for political scientists to use the skill and knowledge of the depth psychologist. With his help they may detect the influence of family structure and early childhood experience in people's adult conceptions of what politics is and ought to be. Ideology can also have a sociological source, as when we detect the influence of economic class in the differing interpretations of the same situation by persons occupying different positions in the mode of production.

Position in the polity can also independently be a source of ideological bias. Governors and governed commonly look at the same situation differently. For instance, according to Karl Mannheim, there is a bureaucratic ideology that leads government officials to interpret a revolutionary situation as essentially a problem in administration.[8] The differences of outlook spring from different positions in the authority structure, and they proceed in part simply from different lines of experience. The politician and the bureaucrat, while acting in the same situation, will have different roles and functions and so will be alert to different facts and causal sequences. Both may be correct in seeing respectively the political and the administrative causes of governmental breakdown. They have different interpretations because they are ignorant of one another's experience.

Yet as in the case of economic class bias, there may be something more. Differing views may reflect an element of interest as well as ignorance. We say we can detect the effort of an individual or group to maintain his or its power position. Giving rise to interest are such factors as personal survival and professional pride. But also and perhaps most interesting is the role of moral and political values: the unwillingness of an individual—or group, or party, or political class, whether governors or governed—to admit some factual state of affairs because according to their value system it ought not to exist. In this sense the democrat is as reluctant to admit that the people may be corruptible as the aristocrat that his class may be decadent. Again, when a political scientist simply lays out some empirically substantiated proposition about political behavior on a sensitive subject, he may be violently attacked as wicked by people whose ideology includes the denial of this proposition.

Finally, in this brief suggestion of the many sources of ideological bias, we should mention the methodological source. By this is meant the possibility that in some degree a value commitment is inevitable in the process of conceptual thought itself. I say possibility because this is a complex and contested question among philosophers, which makes it feasible in this context only to sketch the problem. The problem centers around what is called the "inductive leap" in scientific inquiry. The main object of such inquiry is to arrive at general laws that make prediction possible with a high degree of statistical probability. The basis for generalization is the observed sequence of antecedent and consequent in numerous instances. How many such repetitions must occur before the observer has "enough" to justify his predicting that the sequence will recur with a certain probability?

---

[8]See Karl Mannheim's discussion of bureaucratic conservatism in his *Ideology and Utopia: an Introduction to the Sociology of Knowledge* (New York, 1936), pp. 104–106.

In reply to this question the observer might say that he relies upon a general law derived from previous experience regarding the necessary empirical basis for successful prediction. Having found that in the past a certain number of repetitions has sufficed to provide a ground for prediction, he applies this rule to his present inquiry. Needless to say, this general law itself remains unvalidated, since it presupposes a convincing answer to the question of "how many is enough." Induction alone cannot validate induction.

For reasons such as these, "the theory of Induction" is, in Alfred North Whitehead's words, "the despair of philosophy."[9] Yet people do go ahead generalizing from past experience and, moreover, offering predictions and basing action on such predictions. In so doing they are making what is called an "inductive leap," that is, adding something to inquiry not itself strictly derivable from induction. The force impelling them to make this leap and guiding them while making it would seem to be some value preference. Ideally, perhaps, pure science can wait, holding belief in suspension indefinitely through all mutations of the data. Purposive men, however, must act for goals and according to standards. But since the data will always be in some degree inconclusive, they would remain suspended in inaction unless at some point they made an ethical commitment.

The practical effects of this methodological problem are only too easy to observe. Since we have no rule of "how many is enough," the way is open for ideological choice. When we do not like the generalization experience seems to indicate, we ask for more data and prolong the inquiry. When results conform to preferences, on the other hand, our inclination is not to waste time in further research. To the behavior of the men—or parties or nations—that we feel are on our side, we do not apply quite the same stringent reality tests as those by which we try our enemies and opponents.

Moreover, while the problem of the "inductive leap" applies to any type of scientific inquiry, it is more acute in some fields than others. In physical science the uniformities are massively dependable in comparison with the data with which the political scientist must work. Uniformities in political behavior can be detected. Their ratio of statistical probability, however, will be relatively low. Also, the generalizations of political science are not only in this sense "soft" in relation to uniformities of behavior; they also depend heavily upon a changing historical context. This means that even such generalizations as political science achieves may well be invalidated as new uniformities emerge in the course of historical development. For one reason or another, in political analysis the gap between data and generalization is only too often a veritable abyss. If the political scientist

---

[9] Alfred North Whitehead, *Science and the Modern World* (New York, 1935), p. 35.

is to bridge this gap and conclude his inquiry with success, the temptation is very great to rely upon some ethical or ideological commitment to buoy him up as he reaches from wobbly data toward firm conclusions. If political science is rarely "value-free," one reason is the intrinsic variability of political behavior.

Systems of Expressive Symbolism

In a book about politics, it is easy and natural to write about belief systems and value systems. They are rather bookish subjects, the kind of thing we can handle in a seminar, classifying, criticizing for internal consistency, and analyzing for logical implications. This is not to deny their great influence on political behavior, especially in the modern polity, which more than other regimes is built on general ideas and broad ideals. Yet without being at all anti-intellectual, we must recognize that in any political culture there is another whole order of symbolism that is particular rather than general, that bears a heavy load of affect, and that is geared even more intimately into human motivation. While most students of politics readily acknowledge the importance of this level of political culture and this aspect of political action, they find it much harder to talk clearly and systematically about it. Parsons' notion of expressive symbolism[10] is a helpful starting point, although not everything to be said in this section faithfully reflects his views.

What expressive symbols are and what functions they perform can be illustrated if we will reflect briefly on the sources of solidarity of certain small groups, such as the family or neighborhood. Such groups, often called primary or "face-to-face" communities, usually involve bonds of self-interest. In the family, for instance, there is a division of labor that up to a point is advantageous to all. Likewise, common values normally define what is worthwhile and what a person's rights and duties are. But obviously the intense solidarity of such a group (we are making the assumption of harmony for the sake of illustration) is based on something much more personal. The picture of the group that each member carries in his head is not of a general structure, nor of types, but of actual people with names and individual tastes and temperaments. The life of the group consists in the interaction of these distinctive individualities, and the basis of its solidarity is the attachment of each member to their particularities. Adequately to describe the life of the group, the observer could not stop at a report of its cognitive and normative conceptual framework. He would have to give in some detail an historical account of how concretely the group lived

---

[10]Parsons, *The Social System, op. cit.,* Chap. 9, "Expressive Symbols and the Social System: the Communication of Affect."

and worked together. The common culture of the group, in short, includes not only its conceptual symbols, but also an array of highly personalized representations that are, so to speak, condensations of the group's history. These expressive symbols constitute an important level of the group's culture and function to regulate its conduct and maintain its solidarity.

Nationality as Expressive Action

What is obvious in the case of primary communities also in an important way holds true of larger secondary communities, even those very large secondary communities called nations. The importance of the nation in relation to the modern political system can hardly be exaggerated. "The nation," writes Rupert Emerson, "is today the largest community which, when the chips are down, effectively commands men's loyalty . . ."[11] When political scientists analyze the basis of national solidarity, they stress the importance of a common culture, which involves common political ideals as well as a shared outlook as shown by a common language. But they also give great stress to historical experience. Concluding his authoritative definition, Emerson specifies that a nation will normally be "shaped to a common mold by many generations of shared historical experience." This emphasis on history goes back to the earliest students of nationality and nationalism. Nearly a hundred years ago Ernest Renan, in one of the earliest and still one of the most profound works on the subject, denied that the basis of nationality was race, geography, language, religion, or a mere community of interest and stressed the importance of a common historical experience. He concluded his account with the famous assertion: "The existence of a nation is a plebiscite of every day, as the existence of the individual is a perpetual affirmation of life."[12]

The language may be a bit florid for our taste, but it brings out not only the historical origin, but especially the concreteness of nationality as an objective of action. The "plebiscite of every day" is the people voting with their feet as they move through the intricate and particular patterns handed down to them from the past; by this behavior they affirm the national vision.

Not the great historic moment nor some abstract moral quality, but the daily round of interconnected activities constitutes the substance of nationality. These activities have value in themselves, as well as, no doubt, being instrumental to other values. After characterizing this kind of action theoretically, we shall turn to the principal question of its relationship to political culture.

---

[11] Rupert Emerson, *From Empire to Nation: the Rise to Self-Assertion of Asian and African Peoples* (Cambridge, Mass., 1960), p. 95.

[12] Ernest Renan, *What Is a Nation?* (1882).

Some acts are performed as means to an end, other acts are performed as ends in themselves. Action, either individual or social, that is taken for its own sake is called *expressive action,* in contrast with *instrumental action.* In the case of purely instrumental action, the individual performs the act in order to reach a situation in which he satisfies some need. The action constituting the gratification of that need is expressive action. Such action need not be crudely hedonistic; it may express the need to care for others. The needs and dispositions that are so expressed are not merely instinctual, but have been conditioned by appreciative and moral values. In terms of the means-ends-consequences formula, the acts expressing these needs and dispositions are the realization of the ends-in-view that have guided the course of action. "The essential point," writes Parsons, "is the primacy of 'acting out' the need-disposition itself rather than subordinating gratification to a goal outside the immediate situation or to a restrictive norm."[13]

Needless to say, this distinction is often blurred by relativities. Much instrumental action is also expressive. Some people enjoy their work as well as the leisure to which it leads; politicians may enjoy running for, as well as holding, office. Likewise, patterns of action that are strongly expressive and valued highly for their own sakes are often instrumental to other ends. An educational system aims at raising the cultural level of the citizenry; but a higher cultural level also presumably means that as voters the citizens will show more sense in solving the problems of the polity. In spite of these relativities, it is obvious that men and groups and nations do act for some ends and value such action for its own sake. Nationality, as we have seen, consists in such patterns of expressive action.

Expressive Symbolism

Members of a political system not only act out the patterns of expressive action, but they also talk about them. Or to put the matter more broadly and accurately, they refer to these patterns of action by systems of symbols. The symbol systems include cognitive and normative maps. But people also refer to the patterns of expressive action by means of another level of political culture consisting of systems of expressive symbols.

A first characteristic of these symbols is their particularity, corresponding to the particularity of the expressive action to which they refer. They are typically the stories, legends, folklore, heroic examples, and popular histories by which a nation—or an ethnic community, or other solidary group—pictures itself to itself. Just as history as the sequence of concrete and unique events is the main source of patterns of expressive action, so history as historiography, the account of what supposedly happened, is a

---

[13]Parsons, *The Social System, op. cit.,* p. 384.

principal type of expressive symbol. Both the normative-cognitive symbol and the expressive symbol are regulative mechanisms of the political culture; both condition action in the political system. But they operate differently, one teaching by precept, the other by example. Nor can the latter be reduced to the former. On the contrary, generalities are notoriously ambiguous, depending upon illustration and example to clarify their meanings. Moreover, examples may influence behavior directly and without being reduced to a rule by the person acting. The person acting may be quite decisive, yet be unable to reduce the meaning of his act to a rule or to describe conceptually what he is doing.

A political culture, in short, will normally include an order of symbols that functions in this particularistic way, not only to describe but also to regulate action. Students of political culture should recognize—as some emphatically do—that there are severe limits to a survey of attitudes that asks only for general answers to general questions. Subjects of such an inquiry may seem uninformed, uninterested, and downright stupid simply because the inquirer has not reached for the right level of political symbolism.

The importance as well as the complexity of expressive symbols is heightened by the fact that they include complex patterns of action. Ceremonies are an obvious case. A May Day parade in Moscow, for instance, with its contingents from trade unions, ethnic groups, sports organizations, and the various armed services, is a representation or symbol of the national life (according to the orthodox view). It says by means of action what could also be said in words in a patriotic speech; but the parade says it much more effectively because of the heightened emotional impact of action, especially mass action, in contrast with mere words. Such ceremonies, common to all countries, teach by example, but by example acted out. As symbols they refer in various ways to the polity, presumably strengthening its authority structure and common purpose. Ceremonial occasions are themselves instances of expressive action, patterned social behavior performed for its own sake. By means of them commitment to a regime is acted out and so is revived and reinforced.

In most political systems, a great deal of behavior has such a symbolic aspect and function, even when not nominally ceremonial. When, for instance, a Member of Parliament rises in his place in the House of Commons and puts his question to a Minister at Question Time, he is seeking, say, to bring out some error of administration, to show the superiority of his party's position, or to demonstrate his own dialectical skill. This is the instrumental aspect of his action. At the same time, this act of participation expresses an attitude toward the House, an attitude of acceptance and identification. It is part of a play, a secular liturgy, put on for the benefit not only of members, but also the outside world—to show them in little how Britain is governed.

It is essential, of course, that the behavior conform to the House of Commons manner. Speakers should not be unintentionally rude; their tone of discourse should be conversational, and the general style of speech and behavior should conform not only to the rules of procedure of the House and its conventions, but also to a complex of examples and precedents that could never be reduced to a code. Unspoken though these criteria may be, they constitute a rigorous discipline and perform an important function. In political speech as in rhetoric generally, style must fit content if communication is to be effective. But how can someone call for a revolution and echo the cries of a distressed proletariat when standing in a back row without a desk to pound or a tribunal from which to orate and addressing a class enemy as "the Right Honorable Gentleman"? It is no wonder that, as Aneurin Bevan remarked, the House of Commons "softens the acerbities of class feeling."

As this discussion suggests, a principal function of expressive symbolism is to facilitate identification. The roots of identification are psychological—indeed, according to Sigmund Freud, they are basically sexual[14]—and add powerful undergirding to human communities. The object with which the individual identifies may be a nation, an ideological movement, a party, ethnic community, or other solidary group. To say that identification occurs with solidary groups is simply to take note of two aspects of the same process. Identification is essentially an emotional bond, a sense of belonging, which thereby creates a solidary relation with the group. A solidary relation stands in contrast with relations resulting from calculations of interest, as in the case of employer and employee, and with relations resulting from agreement on an ideal, as in the case of membership in a pressure group promoting some social cause.

While the concept of identification and the psychological analysis of its roots are contemporary, the vital role of emotion in politics has frequently had to be rediscovered, perhaps because of the inevitably rationalistic bias of most scholarly writers. Among the classic political philosophers few had as sensitive an understanding of the role of expressive symbolism as Edmund Burke. His critique of the notion that the polity can be founded solely upon a self-interested contract or ideological consensus is still sound political science. In his *Reflections on the Revolution in France* (1790) he summed up his outlook in this attack on the abstract rationalism of the French *philosophes*:

> On the scheme of this barbarous philosophy, . . . laws are to be supported only by their own terrors, and by the concern which each individual may find in them from his own private speculations, or can spare to them from his own private

---

[14]See especially Sigmund Freud, *Group Psychology and the Analysis of the Ego,* James Strachey (tr.) (London, 1922).

interests. In the groves of *their* academy, at the end of every vista, you see nothing but the gallows. Nothing is left which engages the affections of the commonwealth. On the principles of this mechanic philosophy our institutions can never be embodied, if I may use the expression, in persons; so as to create in us love, veneration, admiration, or attachment. But that sort of reason which banishes the affections is incapable of filling their place. These public affections, combined with manners, are required sometimes as supplements, sometimes as correctives, always as aids to law.

Conceptions of Legitimacy

The problem of political order arises when in systems of action that unite men in purposive action some men give orders to others. A basic hypothesis of the approach to politics taken in this book is that we cannot explain with regard to some particular system how this problem is solved—or fails to be solved—without an understanding of the political culture of the system. Structures of political domination owe their stability and continuity significantly to the support they receive from systems of belief, values, and expressive symbolism. Such supportive cultural patterns can be called conceptions of legitimacy. To an important extent these shared elements of political culture lead the governed to obey because they feel an obligation to obey and the governors to command because they feel a right and duty to do so. In this way political culture may legitimize, shape, and stabilize the command-obedience relations of a polity.

These assertions can be clarified and developed and their conflict with other major perspectives on politics brought out if we take up some of the objections. The first, which is perhaps also the most ancient, is that domination in a polity depends not upon shared values, but simply upon force. If the polity is not merely a holdup, it is an institutionalized holdup. "Without justice," asked St. Augustine, "what are kingdoms but great robberbands?"

Two points need to be made in reply. First, it must be granted that any survey of polities in time or space will turn up more than a fair number of instances of one body of men holding another body of men in subjection primarily through force and violence. The Nazi occupation of various countries in Europe would start off the list with a substantial number of entries. Indeed, the territorial boundaries of any polity will contain some persons whose relation to the polity is essentially determined by force.

The fact that one body of men may hold another body in subjection, however, diverts attention from the real political problem, which reappears in the relations of command and obedience in the governing body itself. That body can exercise force against the other only because it is an action system within which domination is based on more than force. In this sense, as David Hume pointed out, force ultimately rests on opinion. Persons who are dominated solely by force are not related to the polity as members of it but as objects of it. Such a class of polities would be "tax-gathering states," such as the Mogul empire in India, which, resting on conquest, established a regularized system of tribute and otherwise left the subject peoples free to follow their own ways.

Another objection arises when human action is considered from an economic perspective. Where there is free exchange, command-obedience relations also arise. A buyer puts in an order at the store; the employer orders the employee to do some piece of work. In this economic model, however, the power to issue orders is based neither upon force nor upon legitimacy, but upon a material quid pro quo. Theoretically, the bargainers are equal, and one party has only the power to order the other to perform his part of the contract that comes from the threat that he will not perform his own; enlightened self-interest sustains the structure of domination. Students of politics from philosophers of the social contract and utilitarian schools to the "political economists" of today would argue that enlightened self-interest is a sufficient bond to account for the stability of polities.

It cannot be denied that self-interest, material and otherwise, is often a significant incentive in support of political structures. In the modern polity the stress on output and performance makes the satisfaction of citizen expectations especially important in explaining acceptance or rejection of the system. Yet, analytically, it seems impossible that a mere balance of interests could account for the continuance of a political order, and empirically and historically legitimacy has always been an important influence.

A third objection arises from a psychological approach to politics. The explanation of command-obedience relations is found at the level of unconscious motivation rather than rational calculation of self-interest or conscious compliance with norms. Early childhood experiences with parental authority have profound influence in laying the groundwork for adult attitudes toward government. Political identification with a nation, party, or ethnic group is rooted in psychological mechanisms developed in infancy. To admit the role of such forces and, indeed, to insist on their importance is not to say that they are by themselves sufficient wholly to determine action. The mechanisms of identification may derive ultimately from infant sexuality, but what the individual identifies with—whether tribe or nation, revolutionary leader or traditional monarch—will depend also upon what kind of polity and political culture he is born into. Psychology has not reached the point where it can explain away conscious motivation based on beliefs and values or the structural determinants arising out of the historical situation.

So much for three major lines of criticism of the model of a polity put forward in this book. By contrast they serve to bring out its significance. Also, as major hypotheses explanatory of the strength and weakness of domination, they point out forces that may be present alongside political values. Such forces may work with political values, or work against them. Loyalty to a political system is enhanced if it is seen by its members as an essential condition of their material well-being. On the other hand, economic incentives can undermine support for a polity, as when the growth of a market turns loyalties from local and regional governments to the jurisdiction responsible for the wider economy. Whatever the role of these other forces, however, the political relationship gains its special character from values conferring legitimacy.

In normal usage, the term legitimacy refers to the status of a child born in wedlock and therefore having full filial rights and obligations. By extension it is used to refer to the fact that something is in accord with established legal forms or requirements, or more broadly, with recognized rules and principles, as in the phrase "legitimate drama." Thus, under hereditary monarchy, the legitimacy of the heir was crucial to establishing his right to rule and the obligation of subjects to obey. Where primogeniture prevailed, the elder son could claim to be the legitimate heir against his juniors, as when the supporters of the elder against the younger branch of the Bourbon monarchy in nineteenth-century France called themselves Legitimists.

Authority and Purpose

The term legitimacy acquired an even broader and deeper meaning when the years succeeding the French Revolution in Europe raised the question of not merely who was the rightful heir to the monarchy, but whether monarchy itself was a legitimate form of rule. The questions can be grouped under two main headings, *conceptions of authority* and *conceptions of purpose*. The first question is who or what has authority. That is, when do orders, such as those embodied in a system of laws, carry with them the obligation of obedience on the part of the members of the polity? Does such authority flow from the will of the king? Or do governments derive "their just powers from the consent of the governed"? The constitution writing that has punctuated the history of so many countries since the late eighteenth century has attempted many answers to this question. The concern of these attempts was not with the content of the commands of government, the substance of the law, but rather with procedure: How were laws to be made and especially how were the persons who made the laws to be chosen? In monarchic Europe, parties seeking change advocated such reforms as the restriction of the royal veto, the creation of elected legislatures where they did not exist, the expansion of their powers where they did, the division of the legislative body into two houses, the extension of the suffrage, and the liberalizing of rights of free speech and political association. These proposals, broadly concerned with procedures, reflect the concern of modern constitutionalism with the problem of authority.

As the political controversies of the time show, the question of legitimacy also involves the purpose of the regime. Parties had differing ideas of the legitimate social order that the polity was to serve. The movement from the controlled economy of mercantilist days to the freer economy of laissez faire was a source of conflict, as well as the occasion for the liberalizing of the structure of authority. Indeed, the "liberals" of the early nineteenth century were at once champions of a rather more popular government and of a free economy and society, as the constitutions they drafted show by their protection of religious toleration, civil liberty, and private property. Modern constitutionalism has been concerned with substance as well as procedure.

Legitimacy is conferred by conformity with the fundamental purposes of the polity as well as by conformity with the accepted structure of authority. Conversely, legitimacy can be strained in either of two ways. A polity can show the most scrupulous regard for constitutional procedures and yet alienate its members by disregarding their fundamental rights. Similarly, it may, with perhaps the best will in the world, take action to promote human welfare, yet act in so arbitrary and irregular a way as to spread confusion and distrust among the people. Legitimacy can be strained by disregard of procedure or substance, the norms of authority or the goals of common purpose.

In a modern political order, conceptions of legitimacy relate mainly to the policy-making process—what I have called the pattern of interests. Norms of authority lay down how these decisions are to be made; definitions of common purpose set out broadly what they should and should not be. Written constitutions, while often a less than accurate guide to conceptions of legitimacy, show the same emphasis in their concerns. They usually set forth the extent and rights of the electorate and the organization and powers of the main branches of government—legislative, executive, and judicial. These systems of rules are at once positive and negative. They say who and what shall have certain functions and also, at least implicitly, that others shall not have them.

Normally, certain limits on what government may do will also be specified—typically, in the form of protections of civil liberties. But there will be a fairly clear indication of what the power of government is to be used for. For example, the long and detailed list of powers of the two levels of government, state and federal, in the Bonn constitution makes clear the broad scope and the general fields of governmental action. In recent years, moreover, constitutions often include statements of rights of citizens and duties of government that require extensive positive action, such as social security programs and control of the economy. Modern constitutionalism, in short, is concerned not only with establishing restraints on government, but also with giving guidance and a sense of direction to it.

In terms of the model of the polity used in this book, the interesting fact is that conceptions of legitimacy are much more concerned with the pattern of interests—the determination of ends and the ends themselves—than with the pattern of power—the means and the process by which such purposes are carried out. In a people's views of how their government ought to be conducted—as in the usual written constitution—there is a concentration of attention on the first of these broad functions. This makes good sense, at any rate from the viewpoint of the standards of political modernity. The pattern of power, precisely because it is instrumental, should be readily subject to reorganization and reshaping for the more efficient achievement of policy objectives.

Insofar as this is the case, bureaucracies, as leading instrumentalities of power, are more adaptable than party systems, legislatures, or cabinets. The discrepancy also poses a problem: Rapid social and economic development often make radical reform of the policy-making institutions as necessary as radical reform of the policy-implementing institutions. Yet the great encrustation of affect and values built up over the years may make any movement toward adaptation exceedingly difficult. In Britain, as Ivor Jennings has said with regard to Parliament, being ancient is important. It may also be a vast impediment to efficiency, responsiveness, and control of the bureaucracy. The very conditions that heighten legitimacy may impede changes necessary for greater effectiveness. Moreover, the normal tension of a command-obedience relation that subordinates bureaucrats to politicians, is liable to be further exacerbated by the fact that the world of the politician clings to its archaic ways, while the bureaucracy is straining to modernize.

Political Culture and Political Order

When referring to any particular political system, it would be more accurate and helpful to speak of political cultures rather than political culture—as we have learned to speak of public opinions in the plural rather than the singular. The reason is to guard against the term's lulling us into the assumption that any polity must have a single, coherent, harmonious cultural base. Such an unwarranted assumption tends to make political culture the source of order and to contrast it with the forces of conflict, which supposedly come from other quarters, such as the economy. Nothing could be further from the truth or from the understanding of those who have developed the term. Culture is important in explaining action precisely because it causes conflict as well as concord. In most political cultures there will be pronounced differences depending upon level of education—the elite-mass distinction. In the European past this difference was much greater than today, as when in the nineteenth century Walter Bagehot was able to distinguish between the outlooks of the great mass of English people who felt that the Queen ruled and the educated 10,000 who knew that it was the Cabinet and Parliament.[15] In that case, Bagehot found the two political cultures complementary rather than conflicting, their function being to sustain the rule of an efficient elite. In the case of France, on the other hand, the persistence of the "revolutionary tradition" among large sections of the lower class (not to mention the intellectuals) has for long periods in modern French history been a major ground for a continuing condition of barely suppressed civil war. Political culture may contribute to the solution of the problem of political order. It may also be a major barrier to its solution.

By way of summary of this chapter, I wish to return to certain propositions set forth when discussing models of the polity in Chapter 2. There I used some ideas of Jean Jacques Rousseau to put forward a broad hypothesis about the function of the polity. The essential point was the autonomy and creativity of political life. It is certainly not my intention to try to lay down as a universal law that any polity will have these properties. I do mean, however, to warn against and, if possible, to shake the conventional but misleading assumption that the polity can play only a reactive or reflexive role in relation to its social and economic environment. The emphasis on the concept of political culture in this introduction and in this volume should help make the point. It ensures, I trust, that the political scientist will not lightly neglect the meanings that constitute an inseparable dimension of political behavior. It helps bring out the crucial function of political values and beliefs in solving—and sometimes in exacerbating—the problem of political order. Not least important, it directs inquiry toward a proper appreciation of the creative—and sometimes destructive—role of intellectuals in political development.

But what I wish especially to stress is that the concept of political culture opens the way toward understanding how and why politics sometimes reaches to such extraordinary depths of the moral life of individuals. Man is a social animal, and certainly for most people it is vitally important to live in a purposive human community. By taking part in such a community they realize major values of personal achievement and social obligation. Moreover, through the polity they often give shape to these values and seek to express them in action. In this role the polity is not a mere arbitrator of conflicts or auxiliary to economic ownership. On the contrary, as shown by the power of

---

[15] Walter Bagehot, *The English Constitution* (1867).

modern nationalism, members of the polity may find in it a central agency in developing and realizing values essential to their individual sense of identity and significance. Political culture is the system of ordered symbols in which such a people express this developing vision of a common life. In it, therefore, the political scientist finds a major ground for understanding and explaining the conflicts and commitments of political man.

Four
Political Structure

A fundamental hypothesis of the approach to political analysis developed in these pages is that conceptions of legitimacy critically affect political behavior and, more specifically, that solutions to the problem of political order cannot be achieved without the support of such ideal forces. To say this is to attribute an important causal role to political culture. In later chapters on modernity and modernization it will be argued that the cultural orientations of modernity have been crucial to the emergence and development of the structures of the modern state and that the intellectual classes, as creators and bearers of political culture, have been major agents of both stability and change.

At the same time, I cannot stress too strongly that this emphasis on the role of ideal forces does not by any means exclude a role for structural causation, in particular the consequences of political structures. A major dynamic of the development of the modern polity has been its structural (or situational) tendencies, and one of the most challenging tasks of the political scientist is to identify and explain the uniformities that result from these tendencies. The purpose of the present chapter is to elaborate the meaning of the three main elements of structure—the patterns of interest, power, and policy—and in so doing to emphasize the possibilities of structural, in contrast with cultural, analysis. Because of this dual stress, the model of the polity developed in these pages will be called the cultural-structural model of the political system.

The Pattern of Interests

The pattern of interests has a dual aspect: It can be looked at as the process by which the ends of the polity are determined or as that array of ends itself. We may ask why it is necessary to distinguish this pattern as a separate element or variable of the political system. Does not political culture take care of the matter? Conceptions of authority set forth how and by whom policies ought to be made, and conceptions of purpose set forth the basic outlines and limits of those policies. Will not the pattern of interests simply be a faithful reflection of these cultural guides? The answer is obvious. Important as conceptions of legitimacy may be in shaping the political process, a major task of analysis is to assess the other forces that enter into this process and the gap between its actual contours and the ideal maps of the system. In examining the pattern of interests, we try to study the actual process by which policy, in the broadest sense, is made as well as the purposes brought to that process and winning out in it. If nothing more, the function of specifying this variable is to warn the political scientist, like all academic people an inveterate theoretician, to remember reality.

The dual aspect of this pattern—that it includes both process and purpose—has been insisted on. A major use of this notion is to hinder a one-sided concern with power—the fairly common tendency of political scientists to study how a decision is reached without regard for what participants were after and what they achieved. But the very process by which ends are determined will be significantly shaped by the type of ends being pursued. E. E. Schattschneider has laid down a general rule, which is so important and well-substantiated that I like to think of it as "Schattschneider's law": "There has been a different theory of political organization for every major concept of public policy."[1] He derives this hypothesis from a "functional concept of politics"—a type of structural analysis—which develops the notion, strongly appealing to common sense, that the purposes people try to accomplish will crucially affect the way they go about trying to accomplish them. Taking an approach that shares the premise of this volume that politics is essentially purposive action, he quotes approvingly from John H. Hallowell:

> One of the inadequacies of the definition of politics as a struggle for power is that it obscures, if it does not obliterate, the *purposes* in terms of which power is sought and used and the conflict of purposes out of which politics

---

[1] E. E. Schattschneider, "United States: The Functional Approach to Party Government," in Sigmund Neumann (ed.), *Modern Political Parties: Approaches to Comparative Politics* (Chicago, 1956), p. 195.

emerges. For it is the conflict of purposes that characterizes politics—not the struggle for a 'power' divorced from all purposeful motivation.[2]

Not only does the concentration on power obscure something normatively important. As Schattschneider's law points out, it also neglects a crucial causal relationship—that "new policies have inevitably produced new kinds of politics," and (I suggest) vice versa. This relationship needs to be kept in mind when the major periods of political modernization in Europe are being identified. For example, in Western European countries in the past one hundred years there has been a shift from an individualist to a collectivist politics. In political parties this has meant a change from the loose, "cadre" parties of the nineteenth century to the "mass" parties of the twentieth. One reason why party organization changed in this important manner is that during this period the welfare state and the managed economy were being developed. Social democratic parties, for instance, were pushing for programs that were based in considerable part upon explicit class interest and that often required sustained and disciplined political and parliamentary action for their successful enactment and operation. This politics of redistribution involves at once a distinctive type of purpose and a distinctive type of organized political base. Therefore, if the political scientist is to understand the "power struggle" itself, the process in which people and groups compete for authority and exercise it, he must consider what ends the various participants have in view.

Earlier discussion of a model of the polity supposed only a single-step differentiation by which the pattern of policy making was distinguished from the instrumentalities of execution. The spectrum of historical polities, ranging from the primitive tribe to the Greek polis, the Roman Empire, the medieval *regnum,* the modern nation-state, and the totalitarian dictatorship—to mention only a few examples from Western history—displays a great variety of further differentiation with regard to both functions. Structural analysis of these patterns has interested political scientists for a long time. The classic formulation in *The Federalist* papers of the doctrine of the separation of powers as a condition of liberty and the rule of law reflected this concern. Similar inquiries have dealt with such questions as the effects of the structure of representation—for instance, proportional representation; the structure of the party system—for instance, the two-party versus the multiparty system; the structure of legislative power—for instance, bicameralism versus unicameralism; the structure of legislative-executive relations—for instance, presidential versus parliamentary government; the structure of territorial authority—for instance, federalist versus unitary governments.

---

[2] *Ibid.*

A major transition in the development of the modern polity has brought to the fore the structural analysis of certain features of the organization of parties and pressure groups. The shift from individualist to collectivist politics has greatly increased what may be called the degree of concentration among such political formations.[3] Large-scale organization among parties and producers groups, such as unions, trade associations, and professional groups, has been legitimized by new attitudes regarding the proper role of class in politics and the meaning of democracy. Such organizations have seemed necessary to represent the demands of class and subclass groupings and, even more so, to give a solid base of support for the widening scope of governmental policy. These intended functions have on the whole been fairly well carried out. What structural analysis shows, however, is that a complex of unanticipated consequences—or latent dysfunctions—has tended to bring important changes in the pattern of interests of collectivist politics.

Any detailed discussion of these changes and the unintended uniformities of behavior to which they have led belongs in the main body of this volume, under the accounts regarding particular countries. Here I will only suggest some of the tendencies that have been realized in Western democracies, in greater or lesser degree depending upon the circumstances. One characteristic of the mass party that has long been observed is the tendency to produce a new kind of elitism. Because this tendency of political concentration has much in common with similar tendencies of economic concentration, it may be termed managerialism. Another closely related consequence of size and complexity in political formations is bureaucracy, or, to use a more general term, formalization. When we turn to the relations of the massive political units of collectivist politics, whether parties or pressure groups, we find important unintended patterns. The interactions of the great organized producers groups with contemporary governments, while legitimized as advice and consultation, in fact often constitute a kind of bargaining. In relation to the consumer groups constituting the mass electorate, on the other hand, the competition of closely matched political parties tends to become a kind of bidding. One result of these processes of bargaining and bidding is to bring the policies and proposals of the parties closer together. The effect of the structure of the situation confronted by the parties, both as governing entities and as competitors for power, is to produce a convergence of positions and a decline of ideological conflict. This new group politics of the collectivist stage of political development can also seriously impede decisive governmental action. The vast economic power of the producers groups gives them influence amounting almost to a veto over some governmental decisions.

---

[3] I am summarizing here from my *British Politics in the Collectivist Age,* rev. ed. (New York, 1969), especially the Epilogue.

Likewise, the competition for the votes of consumption-oriented voters can prevent parties and governments from taking steps demanded by the long-run needs of economy and society. The new group politics, in short, can produce what has been called pluralistic stagnation.

Most or all of these tendencies—managerialism, bureaucracy, bargaining, bidding, convergence, and pluralistic stagnation—can be detected in the politics of any of the Western democracies. They are behavioral uniformities that flow from certain basic characteristics of the modern polity in its collectivist stage of development, in particular from political concentration and the wide scope of governmental policy. While consequences of collectivist politics, they are, however, unintended, second-order consequences. They do not flow directly from the political culture of the system concerned—indeed, they may be sharply in conflict with the expectations and intentions of the actors. Rather they are second-order consequences of the situations created by the structures that are directly sustained by the political culture. They are identified and explained by structural, rather than cultural, analysis.

The Pattern of Power

Power of some sort is involved in every phase of the political process. But the concern here is with the set of instrumentalities, material and nonmaterial, by which the political-action system works to achieve its ends. The power with which we are concerned is only the kind that may be called "the power of the state."

The descriptive task is to discern the pattern in these instrumentalities and their operation. In terms of the Weberian model, the task of describing and analyzing the pattern of power depends on the distinction between the "administrative staff" and the "supreme authority." In the highly developed modern polity multiple interrelations and overlapping between these two elements complicate the analysis. In spite of these complexities, the modern polity generally differentiates the structures performing the policy-making function from those that carry out policies. Bureaucracies, civil and military, are the obvious examples of the latter. Yet it is evident that the "power of the state" is not limited to them. Certainly in the contemporary democratic welfare state, with its wide and detailed intervention in economic and social life, many bodies nominally in the private sector are in fact indispensable to the effective execution of programs and policies. Chief are the organized producers groups, whose skills and cooperation must be won for the service of policy. The citizen has a role in the pattern of power as a member of these groups: for example, the trade unionist carrying out the terms of an incomes policy, the employer advising the planning council, and the doctor serving in the national health service.

But the citizen also has a role in the pattern of power as an individual—for example, as draftee or taxpayer. Among the resources that make up the power of the state are the citizens, whether organized or unorganized, who are regularly mobilized by the polity in pursuit of its purposes. In the liberal democratic state this role of the mobilizable citizen is presumably limited, although, as in the case of the British defense effort during World War II, mobilization by a liberal democracy may in some circumstances be more total than mobilization by a totalitarian dictatorship. In any case, when polities are being compared, a crucial question is how far and under what conditions citizen activities and resources can be mobilized by government—that is, included in the pattern of power.

If we were concerned with the European states of a few generations ago, it might seem feasible to draw the boundary delimiting the polity where the civil and military bureaucracy impinged on the environment. But today large sectors of what used to be the economic environment have been directly incorporated into the pattern of power by such means as the nationalization of industry. Moreover, where there has not been outright nationalization, economic planning and control have created such close and intricate linkages between the huge bureaucratic sector of the polity and major organized units of the so-called private sector that private bureaucrats perform crucial roles in the implementation of policy. Indeed, in Soviet Russia the ordinary citizen is in effect an employee of the state, if employee is not too mild a word.

While the pattern of power must be conceived broadly, it may be useful for purposes of analysis to distinguish between inner and outer rings or sectors. We may wish to distinguish between the central coordinating and planning ministry and the departments constituting its bureaucratic environment. Similarly, we may wish to examine the input and output relations between the civilian bureaucracy as a whole and the structures linking it with the private sector. In the developed modern polity, however, the pattern of power has a broad reach, including all activities used by the polity in pursuit of its ends.

Among the devices for making feasible the further incorporation of citizens into the pattern of power, one of the most effective in the course of political modernization has been the democratization of the pattern of interests. In a modern representative democracy the voters, the ultimate burden creators, are, roughly speaking, the citizens, the ultimate burden bearers. In theory this means that since those giving orders are much the same as those carrying them out, there should be no clash. And in fact the tremendous increase in state power among the democracies tends to bear out the theory. On the other hand, the increasingly roundabout system of producing and implementing decisions in the developed modern polity means that often the ultimate burden bearers find the policies unrecognizable. As a result, the distinction between governors and governed is acutely felt. This raises sharp problems of legitimizing the massive mobilization of effort involved in the welfare state and the managed economy, which in large part have themselves been called forth by the extension of democratic authority.

While norms of authority emphasize the procedures of policy making in the modern polity, they also relate to the structure of policy implementation. Written constitutions sometimes enter this field. Under a separation-of-powers doctrine, a written constitution may prescribe the differentiation of the law-executing and law-adjudicating functions from the law-making function. On the whole, however, written constitutions leave the organization of the bureaucracy open; and this very openness, when understood in the context of modern attitudes, is intrinsic to a crucial normative orientation of political modernity. The high valuation put on the efficiency of government by the rationalism of modern political culture means that instrumentalities should be subject to constant adaptation for the sake of better performance. In government as elsewhere tools and technology can and must be continually improved. It follows that the fundamental law should not try to fix their structure or operation once and for all but should leave them open to the influences of advancing knowledge and technique.

It is important to see the positive dynamic of these modern attitudes in the field of public administration and bureaucracy. They are as influential as are the factors more usually stressed by modern constitutionalism, namely, the restraints under which bureaucratic power must be exercised. There are strong practical and normative reasons why restraints are commonly stressed. But we will completely miss the spirit and dynamic of modern bureaucracy if we do not also recognize the major place given in modern political culture to heightening state power, efficiency, and performance.

The Pattern of Policy

Like the pattern of interests, the pattern of power has a dual aspect. It can be looked at, statically, as the complex of instrumentalities of "state power" or, dynamically, as these instrumentalities being used to carry out policy decisions. The static view would be a kind of table of organization. It would include an enumeration and classification of persons and material things, along with the skills and technologies in which the men and tools are embedded. Such an approach to the military bureaucracy, for instance, would give a picture of the various missions for which the armed forces were prepared and the types of situations with which it was believed they could cope. In contrast to this static approach, a dynamic analysis would examine how policy was carried out, as, for instance, in an administrative case study.

The pattern of power in the latter dynamic sense is closely related to the pattern of policy. The difference is that when we analyze the pattern of policy we are looking at the relation of policy implementation to a further environment. For example, the policy decision to have a national health service is implemented by the establishment and operation of the service, which in turn has effects upon the environment in such respects as the health of the citizens, their productive efficiency, their modes of organizing for political action in the health field (not to mention on the plane of political culture), and their long-run attitudes toward government in the age of the welfare state. The term "output" catches the meaning of policy in this context. To continue with economic language, we can think of the pattern of power as productive capacity that has an output in the form of governmental programs. These programs themselves enter into further stages of social action, which as instrumental and expressive action are analogous to production and consumption in the economy.

The kinds of questions raised by the concept of the pattern of policy include the classification and comparison of patterns of policy; their development over time; the analysis of their structural tendencies; and the relations of mutual influence between the political system and its social and economic environment.

A striking trait of the modern polity in recent generations and throughout modern times has been a vast expansion in the scope of policy. The pattern of policy has grown in both variety and magnitude, more functional areas being differentiated and the total output itself increasing. In policy as in politics, to pick up a previous theme, there has been a shift from individualist to collectivist patterns. Greater governmental intervention for redistribution of wealth and control of the economy has produced the welfare state and managed economy in the three democracies studied in this book. With appropriate qualifications, a similar pattern of policy can be discerned in the Soviet Union.

In the democratic setting, one tendency of greater governmental intervention is to create leverage over their controllers for those being controlled. Some years ago E. P. Herring stated the point in a striking and widely valid generalization:

> The greater the degree of detailed and technical control the government seeks to exert over industrial and commercial interests, the greater must be their degree of consent and active participation in the very process of regulation, if regulation is to be effective or successful.[4]

Ironically, a pluralizing and decentralizing of power is a likely result of the attempt to centralize it. As a result, in the managed economies of Western

---

[4] E. P. Herring, *Public Administration and the Public Interest* (New York, 1936), p. 192.

Europe, the great organized producers groups have become so closely linked with government as to create a new system of representation alongside the formal system of representation based on elections. The nationalization of industries, even to the point of state socialism, does not solve the problem. For higher authority must reckon with the skill, knowledge, and power of the people actually in charge of industry, whether they are called bureaucrats or capitalists. It is in this connection that a major function of the one-party system comes into play. So long as its own internal authority structure remains coherent, a body like the Communist party of the Soviet Union may be able to offset the polycentric tendencies of the planned economy. As the cycle of movement toward and away from centralization in Russia shows, however, there is no simple and stable solution.

The feedback of consequences from the pattern of policy on other aspects of the polity is crucially important. Indeed, this interaction of other patterns upon policy and of policy upon them is the major reason why we can refer to the polity as a "system": Each of the main variables is mutually interdependent with the others, and a change in one variable will have effects on the others. As the scope of policy grows these effects on other patterns become more pronounced. Sometimes the effects are quite deliberate, as when, as a matter of policy, it is decided to change the pattern of interests or pattern of power—for example, to extend the right to vote or to introduce the merit system into the bureaucracy. Constitution making is one of the more ambitious expressions of this typically modern effort to use state power to alter the way in which state power is directed, organized, and used.

More interesting to the political scientist are the unintended consequences of policy for the rest of the society and for the political system itself. As state power increases and the scope of policy expands, this topic becomes more important. There develops a whole spectrum of what one writer has called "hidden policies." These are not the products of willful deception by bureaucrats or selfish manipulation by special interests—although the groups slighted by them will probably think so—but of the fact that a constant raising of the level of complexity and technicality makes control of the consequences of public policy ever more difficult. To take an American example, consider the huge interstate and defense highway system started in the fifties. Designed to improve highway transportation between cities and states—which it did—this program also had unintended effects that spread like shock waves through the urban centers of the country. In the opinion of one very knowledgeable observer,

> [It was] a program which the twenty-first century will almost certainly judge to have had more influence on the shape and development of American cities, the distribution of population within metropolitan areas and across the nation as a whole, the location of industry and various kinds of employment opportunities

(and, through all these, immense influence on race relations and the welfare of black Americans) than any initiative of the middle third of the twentieth century.[5]

Yet these effects were not considered when the program was conceived, had no part in the project descriptions, and for a long time went unrecognized by outside observers.

The practical lesson to be learned from such experiences is that "government must seek out its hidden policies, raising them to the level of consciousness and acceptance—or rejection—and acknowledge the extraordinary range of contradictions that are typically encountered."[6] The theoretical lesson is that the student of the modern polity must be alert to the massive dysfunctions that are inherent in so complex and technical a system of activity.

Mobilization of Interests and Power

If we think of policy as the output of the political system, it is inevitable that we should also ask if there are comparable inputs. As the various elements of the polity are interdependent, so also is the political system itself interdependent with the other systems constituting society as a whole. While the polity will affect this larger environment through its outputs, it will itself be affected by inputs from that environment.

If we follow our model of the polity, two of these lines of input from the environment will affect respectively the pattern of interests and the pattern of power. In the history of European modernization the classic instance is the impact of industrialization. It brought into existence new economic strata, the commercial and industrial capitalist classes, which in turn put forward a whole new spectrum of policy demands and supported a system of parties and pressure groups to push these demands.

The process by which the needs of these groups were converted into explicit demands upon and within the polity was not merely reflexive but included a crucial and complex phase, which can be called the *mobilization of interests.* The objective position of a class or group in the economy does not automatically and instantly make the group aware of what its interests are and endow it with an organized mode of pursuing them. A necessary intervening stage is the growth of class or group consciousness. Class needs will remain ineffective until they are made articulate and given some form of organized support. In the period of political development

---
[5] Daniel Patrick Moynihan, "Policy vs. Program in the '70's," *The Public Interest,* 20 (Summer 1970), p. 94.
[6] *Ibid.*

that accompanied industrialization, the mobilization of interests included such crucial transformations as the extension of the suffrage, the development of media of political communication, and the rise of political parties and pressure groups. How this took place—for instance, by parliamentary or revolutionary means—depended in great degree upon features of the existing political system.

Comparable to the mobilization of interests is the *mobilization of power*. Industrialization greatly increased the resources, material and nonmaterial, present in the various nations of Western Europe: the wealth of individuals, their skills, and their organizations. Again, this did not mean that these resources automatically would be incorporated into state power. But sooner or later in all European polities the personnel and skills of the rising classes were used to enhance the power of the state in reforms of the civil and military bureaucracy.

This common process of mobilization of power displayed differences depending upon national differences among the polities. And today differences remain, not only in the character of the respective bureaucracies, but also in the degree to which the polity can mobilize the resources of its citizens. Citizens may resist the state by evading such typical burdens as heavy income taxation, military conscription, and economic regulation. On the part of the bureaucracy, failures of support range from the endemic friction between bureaucrats and politicians to an acute crisis of authority resulting in a coup against the regime by military or civilian officials.

A mark of the modern polity is often said to be its ability to satisfy a greater "load" of political demand. The vast mobilization of interests that has continued through the modern period has been a main reason for the expansion of the scope of policy. The rise of democracy, the extension of participation, and the refinement of tastes and needs have been major background conditions for the mounting output and increasing centralization of the modern state. But our model will not let us forget the intervening variable: the mobilization of power. Whether such inputs of power will be adequate to the outputs sought by rising political demands is never wholly assured, but has been and remains a major problem of the modern state.

Economy and Environment

For the liberal democracies the environment also includes the economic system. In these systems, the interaction between polity and economy is of central importance to the political scientist. In the crucial processes of modernization, the mobilization of interests and the mobilization of power, we can trace the emergence in the economy of new classes whose skills and demands often provide the foundation for major steps in the development of the polity. At the heart of this concern of the political scientist with what went on in the unregulated economy is the fact that again and again economic developments have confronted the polity with entirely unanticipated conditions, massive compulsions to which it had to respond and in some degree yield, and which at times seemed to dominate the life and purposes of the polity. Liberty for the economy seemed to mean a loss of liberty for the polity. Freedom of choice in the economy seemed to mean a diminution of freedom of choice for the polity.

Needless to say, the economic freedom that led to the separation of polity and economy in the liberal era is by no means a permanent feature of human affairs. Normally, on the contrary, what people in the liberal order call the economy is part and parcel of the polity. For Aristotle economic activity was clearly subject to the needs and purposes of the polis. Likewise in the case of the medieval manor, the activity of people in fields, shops, and markets was essential to material subsistence. But this activity constituted an integral part of the instrumentalities of the feudal regime, which by law and custom minutely directed and regulated it. These life-supporting spheres of action were as fully incorporated into the medieval polity as their present-day equivalents in any modern socialist regime.

In such cases, the economy is part of the polity, specifically of that element I have called the pattern of power, and it is incorrect and misleading to speak of the economy as separate from the polity, or as interacting with or having effects upon the polity. The huge public sector of the present-day modern state does not interact with the polity; it is part of it. The nationalized industries of some contemporary polities, for instance, do not interact with the polity any more than the bureaucracy interacts with the polity; like the bureaucracy, they are part of the polity.

This is not to say, however, that to nationalize industry or to incorporate the economy into the instrumental complex of the polity necessarily eliminates the old problem of coercion on human choice by unanticipated consequences. The source of the problem is simply transferred from outside the polity to within it. A huge bureaucracy and public sector of the polity now become the scene of developments that continually strain at human control. Freedom of choice continues to be menaced, although now by the bureaucratic instruments set up to serve it. Means still threaten to determine ends, and the "machine" to master man and human purpose.

Five

The Dynamics of Modernization

The subject matter of political science is political behavior wherever and whenever it takes place. The narrower the empirical base of the study, the less dependable will be our generalizations. The wider the empirical base, the firmer will be the foundation for our generalizing efforts. Individuals must specialize; but for the study of politics as a whole, an aspiration to the status of a science is incompatible with parochialism in space or time. Responding to this need, comparative study has broadened its concerns to include all parts of the world. The same rationale compels political science to seek out and welcome evidence of political behavior in times past. This interest with history as past behavior is a concern that social scientists generally are coming to share. Concluding his magisterial study of the 1793 revolt of the French Vendée, a leading sociologist, Charles Tilly, admonishes his colleagues: "Sociologists have cut themselves off from a rich inheritance by forgetting the obvious: that all history is past social behavior, that all archives are brimming with news on how men used to act, and how they are acting still."[1]

---

[1] Charles Tilly, *The Vendée* (Cambridge, Mass., 1964), p. 342.

History as Development

Stated in these terms the case for the study of history is strong. Yet it is a case for the study of history in only one meaning of the term. To study history as past behavior will broaden the basis of fact on which to build the discipline. Like the extension of study to non-Western countries, it increases the varieties of political behavior coming under inquiry and so widens the scope of knowledge. To argue for history in this vein, however, implies that, though past behavior will often differ in many vital respects from present behavior, this difference does not consist in or come from the fact of its pastness. History is to be consulted and used for the sake of difference, but not for that special kind of difference that resides in its pastness. In short, this case for studying the past presumes that the time dimension is irrelevant. But when the political scientists who advocate the study of the past say that the discipline can benefit from the use of history, they also mean that the time dimension is of the essence.

The concept of development recognizes the importance of the time dimension. It treats the evidence of past behavior not as data cut off from their temporal context, but on the contrary as intimately connected with the flow of events in earlier and later time. In common speech, some entity —a structure or institution or system—is said to have "grown out of" or to have "developed" or "evolved" from its previous history. This means that a study of its past is an important way of understanding and explaining the entity. It means that something can be learned about the entity by the study of its past that cannot be learned in any other way.

There is no single meaning that must be adopted as the definition of the term development. The essential question is how useful any definition proves to be in organizing material and directing research. In common usage three notions are often associated with the idea. The principal one is the notion of directionality or trend in the historical process. Along with this go the notions that such directional change occurs in stages and that, with regard to causation, each stage is produced by the preceding stage. Several successive stages of an entity, each caused by the preceding stage, with the whole process showing a trend—this is the distinctive pattern of historical process to which the concept of development calls attention as a possibility to be looked for and tested by research and theorizing.

The concept of development briefly sketched in the preceding paragraphs will provide the organizing idea for the remaining chapters of this Introduction. The first part of the Introduction was concerned with setting forth the cultural-structural model of the political system that indicated the general functions and problems of the polity and identified its basic elements and their relationships. In contrast with this static view of the polity, the concept of development directs attention to change and its dynamics. Specifically, the concern here is with long-run change in the modern polity. The concept of development can be used when studying change in nonmodern polities. As I shall have occasion to mention, the medieval polity also developed in what may be called rather inelegantly a process of "medievalization." The subject here, however, is modern political development, or, to use a convenient synonym, political modernization.

The argument can be briefly stated. The first general proposition is that modern political culture constitutes an orientation toward action that gives the basic threefold structure of the polity a distinctive character, such that we can speak of "the modern polity" as a general type. Insofar as it is governed by this orientation, moreover, the modern polity tends to produce consequences, intended and unintended, which show directionality over time. Furthermore, the modern polity displays not only the quantitative change embodied in these trends, but also qualitative change as its structure moves through successive stages. With regard to both trends and stages, the four polities dealt with in this book have followed a course of development that is similar in important respects. Because of this common course of development, these political systems have not only common features, but also common problems—the disorders of modernity.

The task of the present chapter is to describe the orientation given to political action by the culture of modernity and to show how the structures supported by this orientation produce the trends distinctive of political modernization. Chapter 6 will turn to the specific form taken by the basic structures of the modern polity, relating them so far as possible to the political culture of modernity. Chapter 7 will show how these structures have changed from one period to another, their culmination being the distinctive patterns of the highly developed polity of the present day. Chapter 8 will be concerned with the problems that follow from this common structure and common development.

Cultural Modernization

Since the polity is a system of purposive human action, it aims at control, and its development will involve an increase in the capacity to control. A present-day student of politics may immediately think of the kind of instrumental problem solving that the modern polity practices: pragmatic, secular, empirical, technological. Yet it is of the utmost importance to recognize that purposive action can involve many other varieties of motive and conduct. It can be transcendental and ritualistic, as in the manipulation of the gods by ancient kings. It can be frozen in a "cake of custom"—to use Walter Bagehot's phrase—that validates the perpetual efficacy of certain instrumentalities and permits no adaptation or flexibility. It can be based on a sharp separation between man and nature that makes nature a clearly defined object of mastery, as in the West. Or it can posit a continuum including man and nature in a unity, as in the Orient.

Scientific Rationalism

Purposive action can be detected from the earliest ages of human existence. In a broad sense, the struggle for mastery over "nature" and "history" has characterized human behavior since men first made tools and weapons and established laws. This will appear to be an unexceptionable and even obvious generalization. Yet the point needs to be stressed, since some students try to identify modernity with man's effort to control his natural and social environment. In their view, modernization begins when men first attempt to control their environment, seek knowledge for this purpose, and acquire a sense of human competence. Moreover, this distinctive situation is held to have emerged only in recent centuries, before which men passively accepted their environment and regarded any effort to change it as futile and even sacrilegious. Such an attitude of acceptance is sometimes said to be essential to the traditionalist mind in contrast with the modern, rationalist mind.

This approach must be shunned if we are to get at the heart of modernity. It does make easy the task of defining what is meant by the modern by reducing it to the broad category of human effort to control the environment. But the facts of history and prehistory contradict this conception, making it clear that men have sought to control their environment—in some sense of that word—from the time that we can call them men. Tools, weapons, and laws are the obvious examples, but magic and religion have also been means of control. In this sense rationalism of *some* variety begins with man himself, *Homo sapiens*.

An essential distinguishing trait of modernity is a unique kind of rationalism from which it derives a powerful dynamic. This component of modern culture is scientific rationalism: the beliefs and values supporting both the pursuit of scientific knowledge and the use of this knowledge to control the natural and social environment—as defined and understood by science. A main current in modernization is the distinctive process of rationalization that is buoyed up and driven on by this cultural premise, a process consisting in the expansion of scientific knowledge and the consequent impact of this knowledge upon culture and social structure.

Rationalism has taken many forms. Ancient and medieval philosophers were rationalist through and through, and Plato and Thomas Aquinas have left us supreme examples of rationalist thought—general, systematic, and logically coherent. Much as it owes to this earlier rationalism, science is a distinctively different sort of rationalism with different conceptions of what is meant by "knowledge," "control," and "environment." It is a rationalism that is not only systematically ordered, but also empirically founded, experimentally tested, and oriented toward a wholly secular sphere of operation.

It is this last point that is most important. Medieval thought was teleological. Its search for the laws governing nature and society was hemmed in and directed by a pervasive belief that an objective moral order governed the human and natural environment. In this view all things had their proper role and purpose in a divinely ordered cosmos. All ranks and orders of men, like all kinds of physical objects, fitted into a cosmos that was at once natural and moral. The alchemists, one may recall, thought of the metals with which they worked as "noble" and "base," and when performing their experiments they were as careful to pray and stay morally pure as to weigh out quantities accurately. The rejection of such a realm of purpose, objective to and yet controlling all men and things, is crucial to scientific progress, giving it in effect (if not always in theory) a single-minded concern with the secular world.

Moreover, scientific rationalism is not only an outlook, but an attitude, a propensity to action. It gives high value to the pursuit of scientific truth and to its application in technology as the means of mastering nature and history. "Knowledge is power," said Francis Bacon, one of the most farseeing and forceful of the philosophers of modernity. The search for power is intrinsic to any form of purposive activity. But the scientific attitude makes its objective a unique kind of power and offers a unique method of achieving it. Scientific rationalism has consequences. They constitute the multiple and complex processes of scientific and technological rationalization that are a main current of modernization. The leading example is industrialization, that immense transformation of economic life, which, in Max Weber's words, consists in "the extension of the productivity of labour, which has through the subordination of the process of production to scientific points of view, relieved it from its dependence upon the natural organic limitations of the human individual."[2]

Voluntarism

It would simplify the study of modernity if it could be focused solely on the cultural complex associated with the scientific attitude. Some writers do find the essential dynamic of modernization in "the unprecedented increase in man's knowledge . . . that accompanied the scientific revolution."[3] Yet there is undeniably another related but distinguishable element in the culture of modernity. In the opening pages of this book, while

---

[2] Max Weber, *The Protestant Ethic and The Spirit of Capitalism,* Talcott Parsons (tr.) (New York, 1958), p. 75.

[3] Cyril E. Black, *The Dynamics of Modernization: A Study in Comparative History* (New York, 1966), p. 7.

sketching the problems of the modern polity, I suggested that these problems could be traced not only to the scientific attitude, but also to what I called "the liberating spirit of modern democracy."

It is fairly common to join democracy and science as the twin engines of modernization. For more recent times this formulation is satisfactory. In political development the focus on democratization directs attention to major aspects of change ranging from the rise of universal suffrage in the last century to the establishment of the welfare state in recent generations. Underlying the democratic norm, however, is an even more general and more powerful idea. This other major premise of modernity is most accurately called voluntarism.

The term immediately calls attention to its contrast with the intellectualism of premodern and medieval thought. Medieval teleology was intellectualist in that it found the fundamental source of the moral law not in will —not even in God's will—but in an objective and unchangeable order. Voluntarism reversed this view, making human wishes the basis of legitimacy in public policy and, indeed, generally in the whole sphere of purpose, individual and collective. Its imperative was the phrase that François Rabelais, a major prophet of modernity, inscribed over the entrance to his abbey of Thélème: *Fais ce que tu voudras.* The will of the sovereign, whether king or people, became the ultimate basis of morally binding commands. Human needs as expressed in human wishes became the basis of the "rights of man." In contrast, the medieval (and classical) view held that the commands of the regime derive their moral force from a teleological order external to the human will.

In political thought the old medieval limits on law making were now relaxed. As has often been remarked, the basic approach to conceptions of legitimacy was reversed. While in the medieval view authority was based on law, in the modern view law is based on authority. The Constitution of the United States, for instance, and the other laws depending upon it gain their binding force from the will of "we, the people." There was, of course, some law making in the Middle Ages. Yet in practice it was strongly restrained by custom, and in theory it was conceived as serving an ideal order that severely limited the options open to men. Characteristic of this attitude was the fact that although many kings were attacked and overthrown, the monarchic regime itself was virtually never challenged. Sharply in contrast stands the modern period when voluntarism opens the door wide to continual changes in regime. The idea of an unlimited authority to make law—the idea of sovereignty—is an essential of political modernity.

Such, briefly, are the major premises of modernity: scientific rationalism and voluntarism. Can either of the concepts be derived from the other, or from some further inclusive idea? I think not. Yet there are important relations between them. Both reject teleology; the denial of final causation in nature going along with the denial of an objective ethic for man. Also, they are related as definitions of means and of ends. Modern rationalism incites men to extend their power over nature and society through science and technology. But as we have observed in our opening critique, while science can create powerful instrumentalities, it cannot answer the question of what they are to be used for. Modernity assigns this question of purpose to voluntarism, rejecting the guidance of teleology, religion, or tradition and leaving the identification of purpose to human subjectivity.

This is the meaning of that quintessentially modern definition of the end of man as "the pursuit of happiness." It is as distinctive of our time and culture as was the pursuit of salvation for the Middle Ages. Happiness has no objectively defined content, but is simply a way of referring to the gratification of whatever men may want. On the one hand, scientific rationalism gives a definition of means that is increasingly precise and differentiated in specialized bodies of knowledge. On the other hand, voluntarism makes the ends for which this power is used as various and changing as human wishes.

Democratization

I have said that one of the expressions of voluntarism is democracy. On the face of it, voluntarism seems to leave open the question of whose wishes are to govern. An elitist answer could be conceived that would put so high a value on the wishes of the few that the many would be wholly excluded from power. When we first see voluntarism pushing aside the old medieval restraints, its first champions are not the mass of the people, but the rulers. Historically, voluntarism spread from the top down, and the seat of legitimacy shifted gradually over generations from the will of the king, or of the king-in-parliament, to the will of the people.

There is a certain logic to this trend. In contrast with classical and medieval notions, there is in voluntarism an openness that readily becomes a tendency toward democracy. Perhaps the reason is simply that although it is hard to deny that knowledge of the good, on which premodern conceptions based legitimacy, is unequally distributed throughout society, it is self-evident that every man has wants to satisfy. If we are faithful to human appetite as our standard of valuation, we are pretty sure to come out with an equalitarian view of the ultimate foundations of power.

Given the nature of the present study the relevance of voluntarism to political development has been stressed, but its dynamic has been much broader. A prime characteristic of the process of modernization has been the multiplication and sophistication of human wants. In economic development it is a commonplace that goods and services that are luxuries in one period become everyday necessities in the next. People who thought of themselves as comfortably middle class a hundred years ago would be regarded as far below the poverty line today. Each stage in the prodigious growth of productive power of the modernizing countries has been accompanied by an equally prodigious increase in the wants that people exert themselves to satisfy. We cannot take such an expansion of wants for granted. It has been not only legitimized but powerfully propelled forward by the voluntaristic norm. Voluntarism is a constant goad to the conception and assertion of new wants, for new wants are not merely legitimate, but desirable. After all, the more wants satisfied, the greater the sum of happiness achieved. The voluntaristic norm supports and incites the use of the imagination for the multiplication of human wants. This expansion of appetite has also been a part of the great democratic revolution of modern times, affecting both economic and political development.

The dependence of modern economic expansion upon a parallel and supporting evolution of tastes in quality is readily recognized. Advertising, for instance, elicits new wants and tastes, as when producers create the consumer demand they are preparing to satisfy with a new line of goods. Moreover, this process of demand creation has been indispensable to economic modernization. If people were to return to the standards of contentment of three hundred years ago, the modern economy would collapse. The same holds of politics. A return to the political expectations of that earlier age would shrink the functions of government to unrecognizably tiny proportions. Like the modern economy, the modern polity also depends upon a massive and continuous process of demand creation. Joseph A. Schumpeter elucidates this function of political competition. Referring to the group demands put forward in the political arena, he observes:

> Such volitions do not as a rule assert themselves directly. Even if strong and definite they remain latent, often for decades, until they are called to life by some political leader who turns them into political factors. This he does, or else his agents do it for him, by organizing these volitions, by working them up and by including eventually appropriate items in his competitive offering.[4]

In the polity as in the economy there is interdependence between the processes of rationalization and of democratization. As the power and productivity of the modern state and modern economy increase, a growing and appropriately differentiated demand is provided for the new activities and products being made available.

---

[4]Joseph A. Schumpeter, *Capitalism, Socialism and Democracy,* 2d ed. (New York and London, 1947), p. 270.

The Intellectuals and Demand-Creation

In both processes the work of the intellectual classes is crucial. This is obvious with regard to rationalization, which grows out of the inventive and innovative achievements of scientists, engineers, and specialists in the various branches of advancing technology. But the complementary process of maintaining and creating demands also depends upon a certain type of intellectual. It is the function of this class of intellectuals to shape the tastes, preferences, and ideals of each generation. Among them are the creative minds that have set their marks on successive stages of modernization. In the development of political culture these include such men as John Locke, Edmund Burke, Jean Jacques Rousseau, Karl Marx and Friedrich Nietzsche.

But the culture of modernity has been sustained and driven forward not only by political philosophers. Poets and preachers, economists and historians, have also developed its basic symbols as they bear on the meaning of individual and social life. Percy Bysshe Shelley's famous asseveration that "poets are the unacknowledged legislators of the world" has much sociological merit. At this level of concern, intellectuals deal with the more general principles that inform the norms and beliefs of everyday conduct. They may express this concern in conservative or in radical ways. They may reinforce the symbols of the established order, or they may devote themselves to the imaginative creation of new models of action.

The history of modern culture has been especially marked by the proliferation of new visions of social and political order. From the philosophes of the eighteenth century to the socialist intelligentsia of the present day, radical intellectuals have shaped the political demands of a society that is increasingly mobilized by and for political action. In conceiving new styles of political and economic order these intellectual leaders have shown as much creativity as the great scientists have shown in conceiving new theories of nature. Such styles and formulas, whether old or new, are propagated throughout the society by a highly differentiated complex of roles—by teachers, journalists, advertising men, agitators—that are distinctive to modernity. The developing political consciousness of modern man owes as much to them as his developing power and productivity owe to the myriad of technicians and skilled workmen who preserve the old technologies and apply the new.

Economic Modernization

The previous discussion has sought to characterize the attitudes that distinguish modern Western society from the Western societies that preceded it. I have not argued that there was a complete break. Clearly, on the contrary, there were major continuities. Indeed, I would accept Arnold J. Toynbee's argument that one of the major "intelligible fields of historical study" for the social scientist is Western Christian civilization.[5] What this means is that the continuities in European history for the past 1500 years are so fundamental as greatly to transcend the differences between the medieval and modern periods. The new attitudes, however, which with increasing prominence spread throughout Europe from the seventeenth century onward, did involve matters of very great, if not ultimate, importance.

Moreover, these ideas had consequences. The chain of effects descending from them transformed behavior and social structure, bringing into existence the distinctive traits of modern society. I wish in particular to focus attention upon two distinguishable, but interrelated, processes—increasing *differentiation* and increasing *scale*. Operationally, these embody the two basic orientations of modernity and by their interaction create the ever larger networks of social, economic, and political interdependence that characterize modern society. The general image of this evolution is familiar. Communities were at first small, relatively self-subsistent and similar in economy, polity, and culture—as was still the case with the village and manorial society of late medieval times. Gradually these communities were drawn together by ties of political and governmental activity, trade and industry, education and communication. This increasing interdependence introduced outside influences into the original communities, disrupting their solidarities and at the same time reshaping the fragments and binding them into vast, impersonal, highly differentiated, highly interdependent social, economic, and political wholes. Such, in brief and impressionistic terms, is the manner of creation of what Emile Durkheim called "the great society."[6]

The general formula exhibited in this process characterizes development in many different modes and different ages. Indeed, the Middle Ages displayed a process of development—we may call it "medievalization"—that also followed this general formula in the creation of its own special sort of highly developed society. My concern here is to elucidate the mechanisms of that special form of development that we call modernization—to say more precisely how the basic orientations of modernity were expressed in increasing differentiation and increasing scale and how these two processes interacted to create the large, complex networks of interdependence constituting the great society. The concepts of differentiation and scale can be used in the analysis of social, economic, or political

---

[5] Arnold J. Toynbee, *A Study of History,* abr. ed. (New York and London, 1947), "Introduction."

[6] Emile Durkheim, *The Division of Labor in Society,* George Simpson (tr.) (New York, 1933), p. 222. The original version in French was published in 1893.

processes. Their meaning and their manner of interaction, however, can be most readily illustrated from economic analysis, from which they originally derived. While my interest is primarily political, it will best serve the purposes of clarity to consider first the economic significance of the terms.

The Division of Labor

In economic analysis differentiation is more commonly referred to as the *division of labor*. The eighteenth-century economist Adam Smith, who invented the term, was also the first to explore systematically its influence on productivity. On the very first page of his great work *An Inquiry into the Nature and the Causes of the Wealth of Nations* he introduces the topic, going on to illustrate it with his famous description of the pin factory in which specialization—the division of the business of making a pin into about eighteen distinct operations—increases the productive powers of labor hundreds of times over what it would be if each man worked separately, making the whole pin by himself. Smith argues that the tendency to division of labor arises from exchange, holding that it is the prospect of getting a larger return from marketing what he produces that incites the individual to raise his productivity by specialization. From this relationship it follows that "the division of labour is limited by the extent of the market." As the market is widened—for instance, by improvements in transportation—a higher degree of specialization becomes feasible, since its greater production can now be absorbed. In short, as the scale of the economy increases, so also does the division of labor within it. And as scale and differentiation increase, productivity rises.

Writing in 1776 Smith reflected—and analyzed—the experience of the first phase of economic modernization in Britain. This was the era of the "commercial revolution" when, as his analysis suggests, extension of the market (that is, increase in the scale of the economy) within Britain and abroad greatly stimulated agriculture and industry. The discovery of America, he observed,

> by opening a new and inexhaustible market to all the commodities of Europe . . . gave occasion to new divisions of labour and improvements of art, which, in the narrow circle of the ancient commerce, could never have taken place for want of a market to take off the greater part of their produce.

Smith was not unaware of the importance of machines and made their invention one of the principal reasons for the increase in productivity resulting from specialization. Yet he wrote before the second great phase of economic modernization in Britain, when the industrial revolution made new machinery the principal means of a vast economic advance. Writing after a hundred years of industrialization in Britain, Alfred Marshall in his *Principles of Economics* (1890) still made the division of labor central to his analysis of economic development. Like Smith he was acutely aware of the importance of scale, laying great stress on how "man's power of productive work increases with the volume of work that he does." Naturally, he was far more aware of the importance of the organization of the individual firm. But although he wrote at a time when the modern corporation was coming to be widely used and British managers were making their first large-scale experiments with industrial combinations, he still assumed that the free market controlled the firm, not vice versa.

After another long interval, which has seen "the organizational revolution" and the rise of collectivism in economics as in politics, John Kenneth Galbraith takes a very different view of the role of the market. In his *New Industrial State* (1967) he argues that the classical relation has been reversed, the great oligopolistic firms now tending to control the market rather than the market the firms. In spite of these many differences, he still finds that the division of labor is central to economic development. Writing when science has come even more prominently to the fore as the principal motor of advance, he stresses the role of technology, "the systematic application of scientific or other organized knowledge to practical tasks." Still the "most important consequence" of technology is "in forcing the division and subdivision of any such task into its component parts." The division of labor is very largely derived from specialized branches of scientific knowledge and is carried on by machines. As in the Smithian example, however, it depends upon an expansion in the scale of the economy. Only thus can its increases in productivity be used. Economies of scale resulting from such specialization are a main reason for the creation of huge business organizations and the effort to create larger trading areas such as the Common Market.

One reason these three discussions of the mechanism of economic development are interesting is that they correspond to three main periods in European economic modernization: the commercial revolution, the industrial revolution, and the organizational revolution. The last section of this chapter will consider this scheme and its relation to parallel stages of political development.

Interaction of Specialization and Scale

The two processes of the mechanism of economic development are *division of labor* (or specialization) and *increase in scale*. Smith stressed the division of labor itself as the source of improvement in "the productive powers of labour." The present analysis, which finds the dynamic of economic growth in the advance of science and technology, puts the emphasis upon some step forward in scientific knowledge that, in turn, when applied to economic processes, involves their division and subdivision. Such an improvement in productivity can take place prior to an expansion of the market, as we see in the present phase of scientific advance, when a leaping technology continually presents us with goods and services we never dreamed of, let alone demanded in the marketplace. Hence, the constant need to keep the market adjusted by the cultivation of appropriate new tastes among potential buyers.

Yet the factor of scale can also vary independently. As Smith saw it, a widening of the market stimulates further division of labor. Such an expansion of scale could be brought about by more efficient modes of transportation, as when canals and then railways opened up markets in eighteenth- and nineteenth-century Europe. It could also be brought about by political means, as when the French Revolution through an act of governmental centralization struck down local imposts and other burdens on free trade within the country. Similarly, a change in cultural standards, by producing new tastes for more consumption goods and services, could sharply stimulate economic activity.

The first proposition to derive from this analysis is that *the two processes, increase in differentiation and increase in scale, can vary independently.* Either type of process—for instance, a new stage of productivity resulting from greater specialization, or a new level of demand resulting from a widening of the market—can be the primary process of change. Neither theoretically nor empirically is there reason for saying that one is more important than the other. While science and technology have driven forward the productive power of the economy through new stages of specialization, so also has the growing scale of modern economies initiated new thrusts forward. The fact that each can be and has often been an independent variable should be kept in mind when we come to consider the political embodiment of these two types of social process.

The point is obvious in the case of economic development, which, depending on the situation, may be driven forward by initial changes in either specialization or scale. When these concepts are applied to other spheres, however, this dual possibility is sometimes lost sight of. In Durkheim's classic discussion, *The Division of Labor in Society,* from which I have borrowed a great deal, he makes specialization derivative. Defining "density" essentially as I have defined "scale"—that is, as the "number of social relations"—he insists that the division of labor follows from an increase in density, not vice versa. Similarly, Godfrey and Monica Wilson, in *The Analysis of Social Change* (1945), find that the crucial difference between a segmented and developed society is the difference in scale, upon which, as in Durkheim's account, the extent of differentiation is said to depend. Citing the work of the Wilsons, Scott Greer in *The Emerging City: Myth and Reality* (1962) also makes the increase in scale the primary process of change in urbanization and the source of differentiation of social roles. In applying the concepts of scale and specialization to political development, it seems clear to me that we should return to the lesson of economic analysis and approach any concrete situation with an open mind, ready to find the initiation of change on either side.

The second proposition is that *the two processes interact, mutually reinforcing one another.* An increase in scale promotes economic specialization; an advance in specialization encourages the search for markets where the added product can be disposed of. From time to time, each has taken the lead in stimulating economic development, as when the voracious markets developed by the commercial revolution conditioned the great leaps forward in technology of the industrial revolution, and the rise in productivity in the later nineteenth century promoted the search for markets in the later stages of European imperialism. While each may vary independently, if an advance in one sphere is to be maintained, it must meet with an appropriate and concomitant response in the other. This "functional" relationship does not in itself constitute a causal connection. It is, however, readily translated into activities that do bring about effects with regard to technological advance or market expansion, as the case may be. Such a mechanism of interaction, it may also be observed, is properly called a mechanism. It is not an instance of the influence of ideas. On the contrary, it is a type of process in which "pressures," "opportunities," and "structures" are the basis for explaining the generation of change. The cultural orientations of modernity motivate distinctively new types of behavior. But once these floods of consequence have been sent forth into the world, they interact with profound effect on one another in ways that may be only dimly understood or barely perceived and not at all intended by contemporaries. The industrial revolution, the rise of the factory system, the creation of the great manufacturing city were only in part—in small part—the intentional creations of their time.

The third proposition concerns the overall result of development. *Together the increase in specialization and the increase in scale constitute a growth in interdependence.* As Alfred Marshall said, drawing an analogy between economic development and organic evolution, the development of the organism, whether social or physical, involves, on the one hand, an increasing subdivision of functions between its separate parts and, on the other hand, more intimate connections between the parts, each becoming less and less self-sufficient and so more and more dependent upon the others. Economic development involves such a growth in interdependent complexity as more and more complex networks of exchange join together the increasingly differentiated parts of the growing economy.

In the conventional image of such development, the expansion of the economy is seen as involving a spread of exchange from a limited to a wider area, bringing more and more people into the system of relationships. That did often happen, as, for instance, in the expansion of the European economy to include trade with America in the seventeenth century. Yet it is crucially important to understand that economic development—and development generally—can take place and often has taken place quite apart from any increase in the number of individual units included in the expanding system. An increase in scale consists in an increase in the number of exchange relations. This can occur within an economic system and does not require physical expansion to include more people or more territory. The same number of individual units can be arranged in a simple, segmented economy or in a complex, developed economy.

The terms used in this analysis of development can be explained graphically. Figures 5.1 and 5.2 contrast schematically a segmented and a developed economy.

Figure 5.1 A Segmented Economy

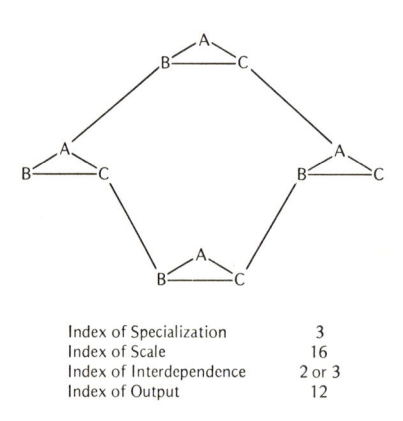

Figure 5.2 A Developed Economy
(Relations of Only A and B Shown)

Index of Specialization	3
Index of Scale	16
Index of Interdependence	2 or 3
Index of Output	12

Index of Specialization	12
Index of Scale	66
Index of Interdependence	11
Index of Output	48

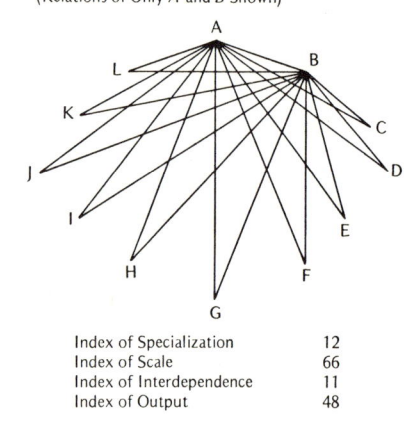

Figure 5.1 represents a segmented society with a very simple division of labor, consisting of three occupations (or members), A, B, and C, as indicated by the index of specialization. The society contains four local communities, identical in number of members and occupations and linked by simple ties of exchange. The lines show exchange relations. The scale of the economy is indicated by the total number of interrelations, 16. The interdependence of the members is slight, each having only 2 or at the most 3 connections with other members. Given the primitive level of specialization, productivity is low. Supposing the productivity of each member to be equal, it can be represented by 1, making the index of total output 12. Figure 5.2 presents the contrast of a developed economy. In this figure the division of labor has increased to the point of there being 12 occupations. The local communities have been dissolved into a single system. Supposing that each individual unit stands in an exchange relation with all other units, the index of scale will have risen to 66 and the index

of interdependence to 11. Supposing also that productivity, like specialization, has increased fourfold, the index of output will be 48.

Political Modernization

The general ideas expressed in these familiar terms of economic analysis have an equally important, though less familiar, application to the study of political development. Increases in differentiation and scale have also characterized political modernization, the upshot being the great networks of interdependent complexity and centralized power that we call modern states.

In the course of political modernization, the dual orientation of modernity has been expressed in the pattern of interests and the pattern of power, respectively, of the modern polity. Scientific and technical advance has made its impact on the mobilization of power, while the thrust toward equality and democracy has been expressed in the mobilization of interests (see Chapter 4). Most studies of the modern state have shown an overwhelming concern with the latter topic. It has long been an interest of historians and political scientists to trace the course by which political demand has broadened and deepened, involved more and more people, and been made effective in the political arena. This is the story of the rise of constitutionalism and popular government; of how over time civil, political, and social rights were made effective. Even where major defeats have taken place, as in the modern dictatorships, there has been an immense growth in political scale in the sense that the spectrum of interests imposing demands and extracting satisfactions from the state has vastly increased. The populations of the various modern polities have grown, but even more important have been the unremitting increase and variegation of demands for new and more activities and services by the state. Like the modern economy, the modern state depends upon this vast and mounting demand to maintain its activity.

Along with the mobilization of interests has gone the mobilization of power, surely no less important, although much neglected by scholars. In part driven by the demands of the groups, classes, and leaders who have constituted the effective citizenry at various times, the modern state has continually developed its potential for acting on man and nature. This story has not been told in the detail it deserves. There are histories of the "output" of the modern state—from mercantilism, through laissez faire, to the welfare state and socialism. But the mobilization of power—like the growth of productivity in the economy—consists in the increase of the *capacity* to produce outputs. Its history is the history of the development of the "extractive" and "repressive" functions: not only the rise of bureaucracy, but also the expansion of the tax system, the police, and especially the armed forces. It has often been remarked that the huge productive capacity developed by the modern economy is totally unprecedented when seen in a long historical perspective. The power of the modern state is no less a historical wonder, reflecting a capacity for policy outputs as vast and unprecedented as the productivity of its remarkable economic system. The centerpiece in this mobilization of power has been the growing capacity of the civilian and military bureaucracy, fed by knowledge in law, economics, engineering, and the proliferating specialties of modern science and technology.

The Power-Interest Dynamic

In political modernization not only are the processes of increasing differentiation and increasing scale analogous to processes of economic modernization, but so also are certain mechanisms. A principal mechanism of economic development, as we have seen, is the mutual interaction of specialization with scale, of the technologically driven division of labor with growing markets, internal and external. In political development specialization and scale also interact, stimulating one another. An increase in the scale of political demand puts new requirements on the state, which often can be met only by an expansion of the state's bureaucratic capacities and possibly by further mobilization and control of the private sector. Thus, for instance, the demand for a national health service, made effective in a democratic polity by electoral victory, leads to the erection of a new ministry, to the establishment of a complex of relationships with the medical profession, and to a method of financing out of special charges and/or general taxation.

Influence also runs in the opposite direction, from the pattern of power to the pattern of interests. In this instance the advance of the instrumentalities of state power to a higher level of skill and capacity stimulates new demands upon their performance. An army, for instance, that has been mobilized and trained for a prolonged crisis may, although the crisis has passed, by its very existence give rise to proposals that it be used to defend some items of national interest that otherwise would have languished for attention. Or again, the reform of the civil service by the elimination of corruption and the institution of an effective merit system will tend to increase the efficacy of the state, and for that reason lead interested groups to see in it a means of achieving their ends. More specifically, the establishment of a special department to handle some field of policy often elicits demands for special programs adapted to the department's expertise. Whichever way the flow of influence, the politician is likely to play an important role. His more familiar role is to represent some interest in the policy-making structures of the polity. But he also often acts to communicate the new ideas and information about wider capacities to a latent public, rather like the salesman for a new product, who brings it to the attention of the consumer hitherto unaware of its availability and virtues.

A contemporary illustration of this typical mechanism of political modernization is the tendency to technocracy. As I observed in the introductory pages, modern government makes constantly greater demands on professional expertise, and the professional-bureaucratic complex grows in numbers, competence, and power. The advances of science and professional knowledge are often such that they can be applied directly to the formulation of governmental programs, as, for instance, new discoveries in medicine may be directly translated into action in the field of public health. Such advances continually open up new possibilities of policy. But they are produced by only a few specialists, who, moreover, are usually associated with the established bureaucracy in the relevant field. From these circles the initiative in policy making proceeds, the politician performing the essential functions of communicating the new possibilities in layman's language to the voting public and cultivating a potential demand for them. The process of demand creation elicits the support of the voters, but the initiative is taken by the technocrats and the primary choice is theirs.

Some of the new federal programs of the United States in recent years provide illustration. The poverty programs of the mid-sixties were striking examples of what has been called "the professionalization of reform." They did not originate from the demands of pressure groups of prospective beneficiaries; on the contrary, as Patrick Moynihan has observed, in the origins of the poverty programs the poor were not only invisible, but also silent.[7] With regard to such elements as the community-action program, the basic ideas and governmental initiative came, respectively, from social scientists and reforming bureaucrats. The beneficiary groups and local and state authorities were no more prepared to understand them than the general public. This created a crucial function for politicians, from the president to congressmen; they had to explain the new programs and win consent for them. One congressman has described this important aspect of the legislator's relationship with his constituents. Referring to the antipoverty programs and other new and complex federal programs, he reported the lack of understanding among the public reflected in the constant questioning by

> state and local authorities, officials of private organizations and individuals on how the programs work. It is more than a question of red tape and filling out applications. Many local leaders may not understand the legislation or see its relevance to their communities. The Congressman or Senator, by organizing

---

[7] Daniel Patrick Moynihan, "The Professionalization of Reform," *The Public Interest,* 1 (Fall 1965), p. 8.

community conferences, mailing materials and in other ways, can supply important information, interpretation, justification and leadership in his constituency . . . These activities of explaining, justifying, interpreting, interceding, all help, normally, *to build acceptance for government policy,* an essential process in democratic government [emphasis added].[8]

A general theme of political modernization, in short, has been this power-interest dynamic, that is, the mutual interaction and stimulation of state power and political demand. The mobilization of interests and the mobilization of power interact to promote the growth of one another. The significance of this mechanism is that it constitutes in the polity (analogously to similar mechanisms in the economy) a means by which the two main dynamic forces of modernization, so to speak, cross over and affect one another.

Nation Building by the State

Analogies between polity and economy are instructive only up to a point. For in spite of their similarities, they are two very different types of system for concerting human action. The heart of the difference is the contrast between *legitimate domination* and *mutual adjustment*.[9] The liberal economy consists of a number of entities, each pursuing its separate purpose and achieving the action it seeks from others by mutual adjustment, of which the most obvious example is payment in exchange for goods or services. The polity, on the other hand, secures action by imperative control, based on mutually shared conceptions of legitimacy. Hence, although both economic and political modernization produce ever larger systems of complex interdependence and although each has processes by which these systems are coordinated, the processes themselves are fundamentally different.

In the welfare state, for instance, the state uses its powers to subsidize programs that are made available to all, or to specified categories of persons. In this instance, the polity is a means of concerting action for welfare objectives, using its characteristic powers of imperative control to finance programs and lay down the regulations under which they will be administered. The program creates a new network of interdependence between those who pay for and administer it and those who benefit from it. In the course of political development, these networks of interdependence, maintained by imperative control, become larger and more complex as the scope of governmental policy is extended.

---

[8]The Hon. John Brademas, "The Emerging Role of the American Congress" (Unpublished paper, 1966).

[9]The term is taken from Charles E. Lindblom, *The Intelligence of Democracy: Decision Making through Mutual Adjustment* (New York, 1965).

These structures of interdependence, moreover, have constituted a principal means of nation building by the modern state. It is well recognized that economic development promotes national integration by increasing the interdependence of the members of a polity. Political development similarly promotes national integration by creating networks of interdependence that utilize community resources to satisfy community needs. The more traditional regulatory functions of the state may perform this function, imposing burdens for the sake of benefits. Redistributive policies illustrate this nation-building effect of political modernization even more clearly. These may involve a sharing of resources between regions, as when an enlightened despot of the eighteenth century undertook military fortifications, civic building, and other public works in the less wealthy provinces of his domain. In more recent times, the thrust toward equality has brought significant redistribution between classes. Gunnar Myrdal has analyzed how these policies of the welfare state and a set of attitudes supporting them have heightened national integration in many countries during the past half century. He writes:

> In internal politics, people can succeed in circumscribing the scope of partisanship; they have a basic level of personality where they think and feel in terms of "we." The national Welfare State has immensely enlarged the number of people who are capable of feeling this "belongingness" to the nation.[10]

This increase in integration, it should be noted, is not only a sentiment, a powerful emotion of identification (see Chapter 3). It is also a fact of objective political structure, consisting in new networks of interdependence created by growing centralization.

Because of its powers of legitimate domination, the polity can achieve objectives not available to the market. This is true of welfare programs that are provided at little or no cost to beneficiaries. There are also a vast number of objectives, such as national defense, education, and so on—often called "public goods"—which benefit most or all members of the community, but which would almost certainly not be sufficiently funded if their support were left to the market and the voluntary action of beneficiaries. At the same time, the fact that the polity's powers of imperative control depend upon generally shared conceptions of legitimacy severely limits the use of these powers. Perhaps the gravest limitation is their restriction within the territorial boundaries of the particular polity concerned. The great strides in social justice accomplished by the welfare state in recent decades have been confined by national boundaries. André Malraux has given the reason: "I subordinate social justice to the nation

---

[10]Gunnar Myrdal, *Beyond the Welfare State: Economic Planning and Its International Implications* (New Haven, Conn., 1960), p. 185.

because I think that if one does not base oneself on the nation, one will not make social justice, one will make speeches."

Modern nation states have shown great capacity for extending their control over ever larger areas of the social and natural environment within their borders. But normally conceptions of legitimacy are shared only by members of a particular nationality. If the polity is to pursue objectives bearing upon the further environment, although it may use force, purchase, bargaining, and other means, it is deprived of one of the principal grounds for its efficacy within its own national boundaries, the attribution of legitimacy to its dictates by members of the polity. Thus, although the economic relations among men have developed to such an extent that we can speak of a world market and world economy, there is no world polity, or anything approaching it. This disproportion between political and economic development is strikingly exhibited in Europe. Economic development has created a vast, complex system of trade and industry. Yet the boundaries of the political systems of the area have barely pushed beyond their medieval origins. Only in recent years have the states of Western Europe made the first tentative steps to erect a larger political system.

Approaches to Measurement

An essential of the concept of development is the notion of directionality, or trend. Directionality, which refers to the quantitative dimension of development, means that each successive stage or period shows greater achievement or accomplishment according to some standard. Economic modernization consists in increases in specialization, scale, output, and interdependence. Analogous processes characterize and drive forward political modernization. In political as in economic modernization these processes are intrinsically capable of being measured, although it is not always easy to find indexes that are precisely accurate. (1) *Specialization is the central process by which the power of the polity is advanced, just as it is the central process by means of which the productive capacity of the economy grows. The civilian and military bureaucracy is the principal field of activity to which this increase in state power can be most readily traced. The indicators would reflect the multiplication and differentiation of functions and agencies that have accompanied the mobilization of power.* (2) *Scale* in the modern polity has been increased perhaps most notably by the growth of participation. Conventional indicators of this aspect of the mobilization of interests comprise data on such changes as the increasing numbers of persons enfranchised; the growing membership of political associations, such as pressure groups; the increase in members and supporters of political parties. (3) *Interdependence* in the polity results from government action imposing burdens and conferring benefits. Measurement of the redistributive effects of welfare state programs would be an indicator of interdependence.

(4) *Output* consists in the actual exercise of the state's power. On balance most modern states have shown not only a capacity to carry a growing "load"; they have actually assumed ever greater burdens and responsibilities. Their activities have sometimes shifted from one field to another, leaving free spheres that were previously subordinated to state authority. Disregarding these differences in fields of activity, however, we can discern a fairly steady expansion of output as a whole.

When this expansion of output is viewed as taking place within a single polity, it may be called *centralization*. What centralization means in this context is that from one point in time to another, a greater sum of the demands of the members of the polity and a greater sum of their resources have been mobilized and related to one another by the state. Output has expanded; that is, a greater demand is being met by a greater exertion of power. In comparison with what the polity did at the previous point in time, it has become more centralized.

To be sure, the structures by which these growing networks of interdependence are articulated may employ all sorts of decentralizing devices, ranging from federalism and functional representation to regional planning and administrative deconcentration. These devices are quite compatible with growing centralization on the part of the state as a whole. It will be useful therefore to distinguish between *primary centralization*, meaning this basic expansion of state activity, and *secondary centralization*, meaning the extent to which the activity of the state is controlled by one decision-making center. Thus, for example, a polity in which all industry was nationalized would have a high degree of primary centralization. At the same time, if it also had—let us say—a strongly federal structure, it would be characterized by a low degree of secondary centralization. The process of primary centralization does not necessarily imply that a greater *proportion* of needs and resources will be politicized—that is, there will not be an inherent trend in modernization toward socialism. Primary centralization means simply that at later stages, in contrast with earlier stages, greater magnitudes of needs and resources have been mobilized to produce a greater output.

Measuring primary centralization presents difficulties but is in some degree possible. It is a beginning to know, for example, how many people with a certain illness were treated by the health service, or how many missions were flown against an enemy by the air force. Then comparisons with previous levels of state activity can be made. Also, insofar as governmental activities can be accurately evaluated in money terms, they can be amalgamated to obtain an index of total state activity and so can provide the basis for measuring changes in primary centralization over time. Rough as such indicators must be, they do constitute significant data, and we shall have occasion to use them in this book.

If we wish to get some idea of the demonstrated power of the state, the problem is much more difficult. The questions now concern the curing, not merely the treating, of the sick and the defeat, not merely the bombardment, of the enemy. Output budgeting in its various forms attempts to answer this sort of question, giving to government an estimate of the actual effects of its programs on the natural and social environment in such a form that they can be measured against costs. Without attempting to be quantitative, historical accounts give impressions of how the demonstrated power of the modern state has grown over time, for example with regard to physical safety or public health.

The growing power of the modern state in its external relationships is even harder to measure. Yet when looked at from a broad historical perspective, the impression of rapid and overwhelming increase is marked from an early date. We can get some idea of the change from the contrast between the military competence of European and non-European regimes in medieval and modern times. The long conflict with the Moslem peoples, beginning with the earliest invasions of Europe in the eighth century and continuing through the Crusades to the defense against the Ottoman Turks in the sixteenth century, gave victory now to one side, now to the other and hardly showed the Europeans to be superior. Then in the seventeenth century the tide rapidly turned. In spite of the brief Ottoman revival in the latter part of the century, the Christian states showed growing ascendancy in military technology, discipline, and administration. Under the Hapsburgs the Austrian monarchy, then in the first stages of modernization, reconquered Hungary and ended the Turkish threat once and for all.

This shift in the balance of power against Islam after a long equilibrium is only one episode in the sudden upsurge of European armed power in the world. As the early generations of modernity passed and European imperialism got under way, the new regime—the modern state—showed growing military superiority over the non-European regimes—tribal, patrimonial, and imperial—that had flourished for centuries. The early pages of Western expansion are studded with stories of the overthrow of ancient polities by relatively small European forces, sometimes only a handful of adventurers. There were the exploits of the conquistadors in Mexico and Peru, the Portuguese along the African coast, and Clive in India; Napoleon's casual invasion of Ottoman Egypt; and the easy penetration of China in the nineteenth century. Modernization brings rising power in external, as well as in internal, affairs. But imperialism, like socialism, while a real possibility, is neither inherent in modernization nor inevitable in modern history.

By way of summary, it may be helpful to conclude this discussion with

Figure 5.3 Political Modernization: Processes and Trends

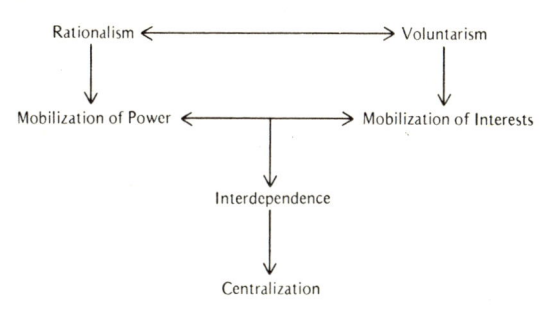

```
           Rationalism  <──────────────────>  Voluntarism
                │                                 │
                ↓                                 ↓
      Mobilization of Power <──────────> Mobilization of Interests
                              │
                              ↓
                       Interdependence
                              │
                              ↓
                        Centralization
```

a highly schematized view of the processes and relationships constituting political modernization. Figure 5.3 suggests the interaction of the main premises of modernity on the cultural plane in the development of European thought. It also shows how this dual orientation of modern political culture is expressed respectively in the two political processes, the mobilization of power and the mobilization of interests, which in turn mutually condition and stimulate one another in the power-interest dynamic. From the mobilization of power and interests flows a growing interdependence among the members of the polity as the expansion of policy shows a trend toward greater centralization.

Six

Elements of the Modern Polity

In two major areas of structure the cultural premises of modernity are directly expressed. Modern voluntarism has produced no more characteristic doctrine than the idea of the sovereignty of the state. Modern rationalism has led to that distinctive type of administrative staff called bureaucracy. The third element of any polity, the pattern of policy, is characterized in modern times by an intense secularism, which has taken more concrete form in the powerful thrust of national—and sometimes imperial—development. With regard to behavior and attitudes, each of these new structures contrasts sharply with the corresponding structure of the medieval polity.

Sovereignty and Bureaucracy

Sovereignty, the idea of an unlimited authority to make law, was abhorrent to the medieval conception of a fixed, detailed, and objective moral order binding on men and nations. In fully developed form, the doctrine gives to the authoritative policy-making organ a superiority to any subsystem within the borders of the polity and, likewise, complete independence with regard to any authority outside. In what is usually cited as the first explicit statement of the doctrine, Jean Bodin, the French jurist and political philosopher, in his *Six Books of the Commonwealth* (1576), defined sovereignty as "supreme power over citizens and subjects, unrestrained by law." He argued that the "well-ordered state," if it was not to be a prey to anarchy, must have within it somewhere—preferably in a monarch—this supreme and indivisible source of authority.

While Bodin granted that the sovereign was bound by divine law and the law of nature, Thomas Hobbes shed these premodern restraints, arguing in *Leviathan* (1651) that "Soveraigne Power" was absolute, indivisible, and indispensable to any viable commonwealth. Hobbes might seem to lean toward one man as the proper repository of such power, but the doctrine of sovereignty did not lack democratic versions. In Jean Jacques Rousseau's *Social Contract* (1762) the sovereignty of the general will is restrained neither by any other political or legal authority nor by any putative moral or natural law. The sovereign people makes law and morality for all its members.

The theory of sovereignty and the attitudes associated with it marked a major transition in political development. They broke from the old medieval notion of the hierarchic, corporate, organic Christian society as a permanent and unchangeable model. Now the regime itself began to be questioned. The issue of the legitimacy not merely of this or that claimant to the crown but of the political order itself and, indeed, of the social, economic, and religious orders became a common subject of political conflict. Likewise, the idea became accepted that the laws and the regime could legitimately be changed from time to time, whether by revolution or reform or by a popular or an autocratic will, depending upon the beliefs of the groups involved.

In England sovereignty in its theoretical and practical meanings—as both a theory of government and a wide-ranging exercise of law-making power—emerged in the seventeenth century. There is a lively and learned argument over whether or not political modernity came to England with the Tudors. The answer depends very much on how we define the term. The fact that decides the issue for the present analysis is that, in spite of the voluminous legislation by Tudor monarchs, the framework of purpose expressed in law and policy remained essentially medieval in its insistence upon a hierarchic and corporate community based on a religious consensus. We enter a world of modern legislation and policy making only with the civil wars of the early seventeenth century. Of this period Charles H. McIlwain concluded succinctly: "Practical parliamentary omnipotence begat a theory of parliamentary sovereignty."[1] But even before these events, the idea of sovereign power had affected English political thought. Early in the century the great chief justice and jurist Sir Edward Coke put the matter in words that became proverbial: "Of the power and jurisdiction of the Parliament for making of laws in proceeding by Bill," he wrote

---

[1] Charles H. McIlwain, *The High Court of Parliament and Its Supremacy* (New Haven, Conn., 1910), p. 93.

in his *Institutes of the Laws of England* (1628), "it is so transcendent and absolute, as it cannot be confined either for persons or causes within any bounds."

In France sovereignty also became clearly discernible in the seventeenth century. In contrast with English sovereignty, however, it was not parliamentary, but royal. While Louis XIV (1643–1715) did not actually utter the words *"L'État, c'est moi,"* the phrase nicely sums up the legal theory of the Bourbon monarchy. "As the king wills," it was said, "so the law wills." Franz Neumann writes of seventeenth-century ideas:

> To both [Richelieu and Bossuet] the monarchy was divine. But the divinity of that institution was no longer meant to imply, as it did to Bracton and almost all medievalists, limitations upon that power. There were none except those that the monarch's conscience imposed upon himself. Divine and natural law were in Bossuet's terms only a *puissance directive,* a counsel lacking *puissance coactive,* the coercive power. Bossuet's formula, *"Tout l'état est en la personne du prince,"* merely generalizes Louis XIV's alleged slogan, *"L'État c'est moi."* In theory the power of the monarch was as absolute as it was comprehensive.[2]

For Russia, Prussia, Spain, Austria, and the lesser principalities of continental Europe, it was France not England that provided the model in theory and practice for modernizing rulers in the seventeenth century. Indeed imitation was sometimes so slavish as to be nonfunctional. At the court of Frederick William the Great, Elector of Brandenburg, that prince, although a faithful husband and strict Calvinist, appointed a lady as "the king's mistress" for the sole reason that such a figure was known to grace the court of the Grand Monarch. In actual practice, of course, the rulers of the time were far from absolute and, in comparison with what states today can do, could mobilize and control only a tiny fraction of the lives and resources of their subjects. It was an age of aristocracy rather than autocracy, although then as later, Russia was an exception.

Bureaucracy

It is often said that bureaucracy is the core of the modern state. The implication of the present account is that the more political aspect of modernity—sovereignty—came first. Once will and *raison d'état* had driven out teleology and the restraints of custom, the pragmatic spirit could enter into the instrumentalities of administration. The new flexibility in ends required a new flexibility in means. If the sovereign, whether king, parliament, or people, was to innovate and reform at will, an instrumentality of state power would be needed that could be readily adapted to new

---

[2]Baron de Montesquieu, *The Spirit of the Laws,* Thomas Nugent (tr.) (New York, 1949), Introduction by Franz Neumann, pp. xix–xx.

needs, given new rules defining its objectives and procedures, and subjected at all times entirely to the will of the supreme power. These properties were lacking in the administrative staff of the medieval state, which derived from a feudal regime that had dispersed and decentralized political and economic power under the legitimation of baronial and corporate right.

Modern bureaucracy provides the flexibility and efficiency required by the new norms. Its members have no personal rights in the means of administration; they exercise authority only on the basis of office. They achieve their positions of authority according to law, which usually requires specialized training and demonstrated competence. Their relation to the sovereign authority is purely instrumental, advisory, and subordinate.[3] Since the human heart strongly resists being governed solely by standards of impersonal merit, no bureaucrats have ever fully lived up to this modernist ideal, not even the superb and austere civil servants of Prussia and their successors in imperial and republican Germany. Some bureaucracies have been slower to adapt to the modern spirit than others. All have shown distinct national differences.

In the early modern period on the continent of Europe the prevailing model was a royal sovereign, assisted by a council and various more or less specialized officials. They directed and managed an administrative staff, which was appointed by the central power and which operated directly in provincial and local as well as central affairs. The lead in establishing this model was given by France. There the principal task of the emerging bureaucracy was to overcome the "appropriation"—to use Weber's term—of public powers by feudal authorities and local and provincial bodies, which persisted in spite of the long history of centralization under the medieval monarchy. This change was largely accomplished between the last quarter of the sixteenth century and the middle of the seventeenth century, the structure of the absolutist regime being completed in the reign of Louis XIV. The principal means employed by the centralizing monarchs and their great counselors, such as Richelieu and Colbert, were the intendants (precursors of the present-day prefects), who carried the royal will into all parts of the realm. Upon this basis the structure of Bourbon power was founded. As Alexis de Tocqueville observed in *The Old Regime and the Revolution* (1856), his searing criticism of the old regime, "all real authority was vested in the intendants."

If France set the basic pattern for the new regime of bureaucratic monarchy, it was Germany, and above all Prussia, that developed its potentialities most rapidly and fully. Herman Finer has written,

---

[3] Again Weber is the standard source for the model of the modern bureaucracy. Max Weber, *The Theory of Social and Economic Organization*, pp. 329–340.

Indeed it is plain that energies as mighty as those which England devoted to the creation of parliamentary institutions were in Prussia turned to the establishment of administrative institutions. While England was founding the constitutional state by the bloody struggles between the Stuarts and the Parliamentarians, Frederick William, the Great Elector of Brandenberg [1640–1688] in struggles as bloody, consolidated his state, uprooted the remnants of feudal administration, and created the administrative organization indispensable to efficient absolute monarchy.[4]

In Britain, as this passage suggests, the new administrative system serving the sovereign Parliament differed greatly from the Continental model. The uprising of 1640 had destroyed the beginnings of a royal bureaucracy that had been created by the Tudors and Stuarts. The monarchy did dispose of the services of some permanent officials—by the eighteenth century the Customs and Excise Service numbered 10,000—and was served by new and growing central instruments, such as the Treasury Board, which had already established its dominance over the spending departments. But the main burden of carrying out the laws and performing other duties of administration was borne by largely unpaid members of the aristocracy and gentry. They served as lords lieutenants, justices of the peace, and vestrymen in the counties and parishes of a still agrarian England. In comparison with the French or Prussian systems, the rising British bureaucracy was small, amateur and inefficient. Yet it would be questionable to say that the bureaucracy was decentralized, if by that is meant that it lacked coherence and common purpose. Once the struggles of the seventeenth century subsided, these members of the governing class displayed a strong sense of their own and their country's interests and, moreover, as members of Lords and Commons, had often made the laws in the first place.

Reformism and Secularism

In this book's model of the polity two of the leading elements of the modern political system are sovereignty in the pattern of interests and bureaucracy in the pattern of state power. As for the third element, the pattern of policy, the programs and activities of modern governments constitute efforts to control the natural and social environments. But this does not distinguish and characterize the modern pattern of policy, since all political systems aim at control of some kind and in some sense. The stress on flexibility and instrumentalism suggests a more precise meaning.

---

[4]Herman Finer, *The Theory and Practice of Modern Government,* rev. ed. (New York, 1949), p. 724.

Modern control in contrast with some patterns of control is continually renewed; reform, adaptation, and reconstruction go on constantly. Certainly this renewal is an empirical trait of modern policy making and of the meaning given to it by the communities involved. At the same time, modern political culture has a utopian strain that runs contrary to this conception. In these utopian views it is held that with regard to important features of the regime and, indeed, of the social and economic orders, change can and should stop at some point. This aspiration appears in the socialist vision of society and history. Yet early individualists, such as John Locke, made hardly any more allowance for the fact that in some circumstances change might become desirable and likely, even with regard to the fundamentals of their schemes. In the British tradition the first political philosopher fully to accept change as an object of state policy was Edmund Burke, whose conservatism intrinsically involved recognition of the continuing need for reform as a normal aspect of government.

Granting that modernity in policy means an effort of control that is continually changing in its specific methods and aims, we must ask whether such efforts of control have any distinctive general character that pervades their many variations. Comparison with the medieval polity immediately brings out the secularism of modernity. Negatively, the behavioral index of this great change to secularism consisted in the growing separation of state from church. As the modern state emerged, it detached itself from the church and from religion, more and more regarding itself neither as subject to a church nor as an aspect of a religious community, and setting its aims and weighing its achievements in terms of accomplishments in this world.

Some writers characterize the Reformation as the time when this act of withdrawal took place and hence as the origin of political modernity. But, again, as with sovereignty and bureaucracy, it is the seventeenth century that marks the clear emergence of secularism as the dominating theme of policy. Religious toleration in law and in practice is a primary indicator. In France, the Edict of Nantes (1598) granting toleration to Protestants constitutes a beginning, in spite of the later efforts to turn back, as in the revocation of 1685. In Britain, while the Toleration Act of 1689 applied only to Protestants not conforming to the Church of England, the spirit of the times also secured a considerable degree of freedom of religious worship for Roman Catholics. With regard to Germany, the termination of the Thirty Years War (1618–1648) by the formula of *cujus regio ejus religio* marked a fundamental break with the centuries-long commitment of the European peoples to the principle that a major, if not the major, task of organized society was to protect and propagate the correct religious faith and form of worship. Again Russia was an exception, seeming to maintain the medieval commitment in its toleration of only a single faith—unless the slavish subjection of the Orthodox church to the state by Peter the Great

88   Elements of the Modern Polity

(1682–1725) is seen as a kind of secularization of religion for the sake of nation building.

Modernity, however, is not just the rejection of medievalism. It has its positive themes. One is the pursuit of happiness. But apart from its negation of the old transcendent aspirations, happiness is an empty guide to collective, as well as individual, behavior. Hedonism may be deeply modern, but as a proposed description of the rationale of modern policy, it does not much help the political scientist to identify the themes that have given coherence to the diverse activities of the modern state.

A more serious possibility is capitalism. It has often been argued that in Western Europe—and the farther west, the more this is true—the emergence of the modern state came about at the same time as the transition to a new individualist economy. This economy was based on individually owned property, which was used to pursue profit by means of a free market in goods and labor. Moreover, it is said, the function of the state was to protect and promote this mode of production and the interests of the owners.

This general hypothesis has added immensely to the understanding of early modern history. Its basic flaw is that it is too narrow to cope with the meaning and consequences of modernity. Modernity embraces both socialism and capitalism, collectivism and individualism. Soviet Russia, with a socialist economy, is a modern state, as are Germany, France, and Britain with their capitalist economies. To refer to all four as modern is not to deny vital differences. But the identities among these modern states, with regard to basic elements, course of development, and virtues and vices, make comparison fruitful—and this book possible.

The modern state has served and has been served by various types of economy. Its main traits of structure and development have not been a mere reflection of an autonomously developing economy, but, on the contrary, have displayed their own dynamic, often dictating the course of economic development itself. As Charles Tilly has pointed out, the rise of the capitalist economy did not consist merely in the release of a "natural" force, but represented, rather, a deliberate choice by the state and the groups controlling it to undermine peasant communities, to break up local networks of exchange, to nationalize the distribution of food, and in other ways to give a distinctive direction to economic development.[5] To put the point quite sharply: Capitalism did not just develop blindly but was "invented" and imposed upon a premodern economy by the political action of the early modern state.

Moreover, not only are individualism and collectivism both compatible with modernity, but in thought and practice they both came forward in the

---

[5] Charles Tilly, "Food Supply and Public Order in Modern Europe" in Tilly (ed.), *The Building of States in Western Europe* (forthcoming, Princeton University Press).

very early stages of modernization. In English political thought a current of economic collectivism has run strongly at least since the days of those early prophets of communism, Gerrard Winstanley and the Diggers of the era of the civil wars. As for actual patterns of policy, during the age of mercantilism, which stretched from the sixteenth century through the eighteenth, so great a degree of control was exercised by the state that one authority refers to what was the freest system in Europe during its early generations as England's "first planned economy."[6] Later, after liberal economic ideas and policies had reached their peak in the nineteenth century, the policies of Western nations again moved toward state intervention, with the result that it is more common to speak of them today as having "mixed" rather than "capitalist" economies. Individualism and collectivism are two warring twins of modernity, and their impact on development has been cyclical rather than successive.

Liberalism is a possible characterization of modern policy that touches a more fundamental level of values. Religious toleration, which arose with political modernization, meant that liberty with regard to ultimate concerns was now guaranteed to the individual. In Western Europe modernity also in due course brought other individual freedoms, cultural, political, and economic. In the case of many countries, the course of liberalization has so closely paralleled the course of modernization that it is easy to infer that they are identical. Yet modernism is not identical with liberalism. Little as we may like to admit it, a strong and highly developed modern state may be oppressively autocratic and despotically illiberal. Under a totalitarian regime, science and technology can flourish, while the democratic thrust of voluntarism is contained by systems of ineffectual participation.

Liberty is a continuing and perhaps unique concern of Western society. It has, however, given rise to different political doctrines as men changed their views of the nature of the individual, his capacities, and his destiny. It was a central issue of the conflicts and controversies of medieval polities. While highly prized, liberty then meant something very different from what it came to mean under the influence of modernity. To begin with, when referring to medieval thought and practice, we should speak of "liberties," since liberty had a different substance depending upon the rank and function of the individual and his group in the organic hierarchy of Christian society. The practical meaning of this assertion is shown in both title and content of *Magna Carta Libertatum* (1215)—the Great Charter of Liberties —which sought to guarantee for individuals and communities their differentiated and appropriate spheres of freedom. Moreover, these guarantees of medieval constitutionalism were not only differentiated; they were also

---

[6] E. Lipson, *The Growth of English Society: A Short Economic History* (New York, 1950), p. 142.

inflexible. For the members of each rank and order of men there were proper patterns of conduct, made known by custom, law, and religious teaching. It was the purpose of the polity to protect and support each member in his station and its duties. For the individual, to be free meant being free to imitate these models of propriety and so to serve God.

Under the influence of modernity, liberalism has given almost the opposite meaning to liberty. It is now the right to innovate, to be different from anyone else, to develop individual creativity. Modern liberty means not imitation of what objectively is best, but creation of what subjectively pleases most. The modern conception of liberty brings us back to the pursuit of happiness, which apart from its negations is an empty category for philosopher or social scientist.

Nationalism and National Development

Hedonism, capitalism, and liberalism, while all thoroughly secular, are either too broad or too narrow to characterize the overriding theme of the pattern of policy of the modern state. We get much closer to a viable and meaningful generalization with nationalism or—if that term has acquired too pejorative a connotation—nation building and national development. The relation of nationality and modernity is a question of the first importance. It has two major aspects. On the one hand, nationality stands in relation to the modern state as something "given," something derived from a source outside of and, indeed, usually antecedent to modernity. On the other hand, modernization has affected nationality, the development of the nation having been the central object of policy in most modern states.

The modern state is commonly referred to as the modern nation-state, and few if any modern states have managed to survive without a basis in common nationality. Nationality demonstrates this powerful function perhaps most vividly in the limitations it sets on the effectiveness of the modern state. In many parts of the world, there are compelling economic, social, and strategic reasons for much larger political systems. Indeed, we can make a strong case for world government. In the absence of a common nationality, however, little progress is being made in the various efforts toward regional integration. Even the states of Western Europe, although intimately allied in culture and institutions, move at a snail's pace, if at all, toward a united Europe.

Crucial as nationality may be to the modern polity, however, its origins are very often premodern. The various nationalities of Europe descend from the Middle Ages. It was the rising national monarchies of the thirteenth century that finally brought about the defeat of the medieval papacy in its long struggle for dominion over the temporal power. This premodern heritage gave to the European modern state a vitally important unifying force, differing in kind from the bonds of self-interest, ideology, and common purpose that typically derive from modernity. The categories of modernity release energy, stimulate the intelligence, and encourage the creation of powerful instrumentalities and comprehensive organizations. Yet it seems that they cannot themselves create the strong solidary groupings and close-knit communities that we find in traditional societies. The typical social group of modern society, the bureaucratic organization, may be far more efficient, but it has far less solidarity than the typical group of traditionalist society, the tribe, clan, or other kinship group. The nationalities inherited from the medieval past had such a solidary character and gave to the emerging modern state an indispensable basis for unity and effectiveness.

The relation between modernity and nationality has been complex. In each of the four states examined in this book, a dominant nationality provided an initial basis of unity for the political system. Yet this force has not been without rivals within the borders of the state. In the earlier phases of modernization, the strength and unity of the British polity depended upon the solidarity of English nationality, but to this day its rivals in the form of Scottish, Welsh, and (emphatically) Irish nationality have never been wholly absorbed into the British nation. Similarly, in France, which also entered the modern period with a strongly based national monarchy, we still see the force of other territorial loyalties, as in the very powerful regional movement in Brittany. The German nationality also goes back to the Middle Ages. But in contrast with English and French experience, the splintering of the medieval German polity made the national question one of desperate urgency in the modern period. Today German federalism is a recognition of the continuing strength of regional and subnational loyalties. In Russia, the Great Russians of the medieval kingdom of Moscovy provided the national nucleus from which the centuries-long conquest of the vast empire of the present day was launched. But the welcome the Ukrainians gave to the invading Nazi armies during World War II was an act of national liberation from Great Russian domination as well as of resistance to Stalinist dictatorship.

While a dominant nationality has been an indispensable basis of the polity in all four countries, it has never been able completely to absorb its rivals or permanently set at rest their claims for some kind of political expression. One of the most fascinating aspects of contemporary European politics is the revival of these lesser nationalities as political groups demanding a reversal of the long trend to centralization in the modern state and some degree of political autonomy for their members.

National Development

"States have made nations," William T. R. Fox has said, "far more often than nations have made states."[7] If we stretch the term "state" to include medieval polities, this generalization is strongly supported by European history. As Ernest Renan pointed out in *What Is a Nation?* (1882), the nations of Europe, which first appeared after the fall of the Carolingian empire, owed their character to the fusion of various peoples under the rule of medieval dynasties.

While the modern polity has rarely founded a nation, it has often developed one. Characteristically, modern states have promoted economic interdependence by such measures as the creation of a single national market governed by a single system of law. They have promoted cultural uniformity by such means as a national system of public education. As we have seen, primary centralization as a specifically political aspect of modernization has served to elaborate the networks of interdependence and the sentiments of identification that underlie national solidarity. Given a basis in common nationality, the modern state has on the whole and in most cases enormously increased the capacity of its members for concerted action. Although nationality has usually set stubborn limits to the boundaries within which the domination of a modern state will be accepted as legitimate, within those boundaries, the state has powerfully promoted integration. In comparison with previous polities, the immensely greater proportion of national resources that the modern state has mobilized internally for the welfare state or externally for national defense dramatizes the accomplishment. The income tax and military conscription show what the modern state has been able to make of nationality.

Even for a regime so self-consciously internationalist and ideological in its origins as Soviet Russia, nationality has been an indispensable support and a profoundly shaping influence. The two greatest challenges of the Stalinist period were industrialization and the war against Nazi Germany. In confronting these challenges, the Communist leaders increasingly turned to nationalist sentiments to summon up the energies of the people. "In a period of great reconstruction and of great purges," Ulam says of the mid-thirties,

> the regime was also instinctively reaching for all the elements of stability it could find, and one of the most important ones was Russian patriotism. It seemed to be saying to the dominant nation of the Soviet Union: "The regime may be tyrannical, and it may be subjecting you to all kinds of sufferings and privations, but it is your government, and it is doing it for the greatness of your country."

---

[7]William T. R. Fox, in his Introduction to Amitai Etzioni, *Political Unification: A Comparative Study of Leaders and Forces* (New York, 1965).

Similarly, during World War II,

> Russian patriotism was . . . rediscovered by the Soviet regime to be its major asset, and the natural instinct of the people to fight for their government, no matter how oppressive, against a foreign foe, to be a surer basis of its power than even Marxism-Leninism.[8]

The premises of modernity return only a thin and flat reply to the old question of human purpose. Science can tell us how to pursue and increase power, but not what to use it for. The rejection of teleology frees modern men from old disciplines and restraints, but otherwise the pursuit of happiness is an empty answer to our question. On this vacant scene nationalism easily intruded. Amidst the abstractions of modernity it provided something concrete: a language; a set of tastes; ways of eating, drinking, working, courting, and raising a family—"a plebiscite of every day," in Renan's powerful phrase. To protect these valued specifics and to express them in promoting economic, social, and political development, nationalism gave body to the patterns of purpose and policy. Capitalism and education, armies and bureaucracies, although driven forward by identical forces of modernity, in each country received a special stamp from the unique character of its nationality. To make the nation more of a nation has been—for good and for ill—the overriding theme of the massive and growing activities of the modern state.

To identify this strong, continuing theme of national development is not to overlook other objects of policy. Modern polities have been peculiarly rent by class conflict. One reason was the radical shift in political culture from inequality to equality. When men accepted without question the need for hierarchy, finding its justification in a multitude of religious and philosophical reasons, the edge of relative deprivation in material, social, and political advantages could not fail to be dulled. The growing cult of equality in modern times, however, makes the many actual disparities among men and classes ever more painful to bear and harder to defend. Modernity did not create the class struggle, but it did immensely enhance it. Class and group struggle has been a principal motor of policy making in the modern state. These opposing interests, however, have been qualified and limited in appearance and in reality by some subjection to a national interest. During the industrialization of Soviet Russia, as we have just seen in Ulam's comment, the harshness of rule by the Communist elite was softened by the appeal to "the greatness of your country." In general, where modern states have displayed stability in spite of the inevitable divisive forces generated by social, economic, and political structures, one reason has been the pervasive feelings and beliefs of a common nationality.

---

[8] Adam B. Ulam, *The Russian Political System*, Chap. 3 (New York, 1974).

Seven
Stages of Political Modernization

In political culture and political structure, the modern polity is unique. Beginning in the sixteenth and seventeenth centuries, the sovereign, bureaucratic nation-state has come more and more to prevail in the West. It has not only prevailed, it has also developed, growing steadily in power, participation, centralization, and integration. In the developed modern polity of the present time the three basic elements of structure have acquired specific form as separate elements and as a system. This polity can be found in the four countries examined in this book, as well as in all other Western and some non-Western countries. The specific characteristics of the modern polity can be briefly summarized as follows:

1. Its policy-making structure is partisan and participatory.
2. Its power structure is corporatist and technocratic.
3. Its policy is collectivist in economic and social spheres.

Development by Stages

How did the modern polity acquire these traits? If we take the concept of development seriously, it implies that the modern polity has moved in a certain direction, measurable by various indexes, and that it has passed through identifiable stages in reaching its present structure. The notion of stages itself has certain implications. It directs attention especially to the possibility that history is not merely continuous flux, but is marked by alternating periods of stability and transition. Anyone who has read a great deal of history may be pardoned if he concludes that every historian finds in his period of special study a "time of transition," leaving it to preceding and succeeding times, about which he knows less, to provide the stability without which transition is meaningless. Yet in spite of its difficulties, the concept of stages is not useless. In political modernization, significant periods of relative stability occur when the basic structures of a polity remain much the same, in contrast with other periods when new features emerge and become dominant.

Indeed, in British political development each main period of stability is unmistakably marked by the occurrence at mid-passage of an exceptional lull in political controversy and party conflict. The most recent of these moments in British politics, as in Western politics generally, the 1950s, has been spoken of as marking "the end of ideology." More accurately, what characterized these years, like previous moments of lull, was not the end of ideology, but a consensus on ideology. Typically, a period of struggle between an old and a new political order, often embodied in party conflict, had given way to a time when the new order in some substantial part had been established and had won wide acceptance in the active political community. Between the earlier and later stages each of the three basic elements of the polity had changed significantly. In the case of Britain in the fifties the collectivist polity, over which sharp political battles had been fought for a generation or more, came to maturity and won general acceptance.

Another interesting hypothesis that may be attached to the notion of development by stages is the proposition that the transitions from one order to another have been mediated by "revolutions," meaning by this term at least substantial collective violence by one group to change the regime defended and controlled by another group. The suggestion directs attention to a fascinating subject and plausible hypothesis. Some revolutions have been moved by purposes and ideals strongly colored by modern values. Probably the leading case was the French Revolution with its thrust toward extending political power, strengthening the rule of law, encouraging the "career open to talents" in bureaucracy and economy, and centralizing law, government, and politics. The Puritan revolution in England, on the other hand, is a very ambiguous case. What the more ardent revolutionaries aimed at was deeply hostile to the modern, secular spirit, although the outcome of their failure was a great stride toward modernity. Rather similarly, the Russian Revolution promoted changes sharply opposed to some of its original ideals. Deeply egalitarian and utopian in conception, it was rapidly taken over by the overwhelming urge to modernize of the Stalinist regime. Even more ironic has been the upshot of the Nazi revolution, which, although inspired by romantic elitist fantasies, had the effect of sweeping away traditional social remnants in economy, bureaucracy, and army that had long impeded German modernization.

Apart from such ambiguities in purpose and intent, the role of revolution in modernization is even more seriously circumscribed by the leading part that established governing classes have commonly played in the transition to a more developed modernity. The principal case is Britain, where the governing classes, displaying great continuity throughout the modern period, have managed and in many respects have directed the great transitions of this time. In France the monarchy had not only taken the lead toward modernity in the seventeenth century, but also with the support of part of the privileged classes was striving to modernize policy and administration in the years just before the Revolution. In crucial respects the Revolution carried out what the *ancien régime* had attempted. In Germany also, as Guido Goldman shows, bureaucratic and aristocratic groups from the days of the Great Elector repeatedly took the lead in modernization, often anticipating the modernizing demands of excluded groups by absorbing both demands and groups into their own dynamic.[1] In Russia the Revolution was in one sense an exception to the pattern of development from the top that had prevailed from the days of Peter the Great. Yet once the new group had won power, striking resemblances appeared, as the Communist leaders continued, although more ruthlessly and perhaps more rapidly, the modernizing effort of their predecessors.

In sum it must be emphasized that revolutions do not inevitably consist in the rising up of modernizers against traditionalists. On the contrary, revolution may occur when a modernizing regime falters in its effort of further development. To return once again to the French example, in the eighteenth century the Bourbon monarchy was modernizing, although at a slower pace than in its electric years under Louis XIV. Moreover, it had the support of a part of the privileged classes. A larger part, however, resisted, and the nobiliary reaction, an antimodern move, constituted one of the main precipitating causes of the Revolution. Overcoming the resistance of these groups that had blocked the modernizing efforts of the monarchy, the French Revolution carried forward the work that the Old Regime had instituted and failed to complete.

Such an interpretation, it should be added, greatly helps comparative study of modernization in France and England. If we start with the premise that revolutions are needed to accomplish the transition from premodern to modern regimes, it must follow that both the Puritan and French revolutions performed such similar functions. This is historically and empirically absurd for many reasons, not the least being the fact that France was the leader in political modernization. The solution is to give up the untenable

---

[1] Guido Goldman, *The German Political System*, Chap. 1 (New York, 1974).

premise and to recognize (1) that transitions can occur without revolutions —as in the case of early modernization in France—and (2) that they may be precipitated in the course of modernization by defects of regime and policy—as in the case of the French Revolution.

A third proposition that has sometimes been attached to the notion of development is the hypothesis of cumulation. The contention is that in each stage the modern polity has acquired certain features that have remained in succeeding stages. The developed modern polity of the present time, therefore, embodies accomplishments of previous eras as well as the present era of modernity. The idea does sometimes fit the facts. In a classic essay on the growth of English citizenship, T. H. Marshall has shown how the present conception was built up over a long history, in each of three stages a distinctive and notable advance being made.[2] The seventeenth and eighteenth centuries established civil rights in the legal sense of the rule of law and protection against arbitrary action, as, for instance, by establishing habeas corpus. In the nineteenth and twentieth centuries political rights were added, as the franchise was extended and the rights necessary to make the vote effective, such as freedom of speech and of the press, were secured. In recent generations social rights have come to be guaranteed by the growth of the welfare state.

The hypothesis of cumulation points to a kind of explanation of present structures by means of the examination of their origins. Vice versa, it constitutes an interpretation of development as the successive production of features retained in the end product. In this latter guise, it sounds a hopeful note and could be used to fill out the vision of progress. But applicable as it may be in some instances, it cannot obscure the vast discontinuities in even the most gradual and incremental development. Any historical change inevitably means the loss of things and qualities— the death of persons and the fading of their impression on contemporaries, the destruction of old institutions by the emergence of new ones, and the decay of a unique quality of life enjoyed or endured by a class or by society as a whole.

To hold that there are certain stages through which the process of political modernization must inevitably pass is a very dubious proposition. Human ingenuity, imagination, and plain historical accident have ways of playing havoc with rigid schemes. Looking back over the three hundred years or so of European modernization, we cannot fail to be impressed with how the peculiarities of a country's heritage, its individual leadership, and the odd conjunctures of events have served to impress unique and lasting marks on its polity.

Yet with all due qualification, we can still see significant similarities in

---

[2] T. H. Marshall, *Class, Citizenship and Social Development* (New York, 1965).

the sequence of phases through which the four countries have passed. Broadly speaking, there are three stages: the aristocratic, the liberal, and the collectivist. Since some nations have modernized sooner and more rapidly than others, the dates for each stage are not the same for all countries. Very roughly, if the seventeenth century saw the beginning of modernization, the eighteenth was the age of aristocracy, the nineteenth was the age of liberal democracy, and the twentieth has been the age of collectivism. The general pattern is that in each nation in each stage there is a stable and distinctive complex of structures that in certain fundamental respects resembles those of other nations in the same stage.

The Aristocratic Stage

The term "aristocratic stage" becomes more appropriate as we pass from East to West. In England this was the age of the Whig aristocracy. Great landowners, descendants in many cases of families who had fought the Stuarts, they dominated the coalition of governing classes and had allies among the gentry and mercantile strata. Under this leadership, these classes, a minuscule proportion of the total population, governed the country through Parliament and the dispersed amateur bureaucracy of the time. Although modernizing, it was by no means an egalitarian regime. Because of the decline in the number of small landowners, the electorate had probably diminished as compared with what it had been in the seventeenth century. The ghastly treatment of the poor and the lower classes, while it had begun to call forth a humanitarian protest, still prevailed generally. Yet Whig constitutionalism, in the name of the Revolution of 1688, established English liberty on so firm a foundation as to win the admiration of enlightened minds on the Continent, such as Montesquieu and Voltaire, initiating the attempts at imitation that have lasted into recent times.

It was not only constitutionalism and liberty that won this admiration, but also prosperity and especially power. The Whigs were nation builders and empire builders of genius and vision. Although economically based mainly in land, they perceived the British interest in an expanding commerce. Sharing the premises of mercantilism common throughout Europe in their day, they constructed an elaborate protective system and by diplomacy and war supported colonial and commercial aggrandizement. Although the system has been called "parliamentary Colbertism,"[3] it did not extend to the detailed regulation of the internal economy attempted in France. Yet in Britain, as elsewhere, the purpose of mercantilist policy was to foster home production, native shipping, and ultimately national

---

[3]William Cunningham, *The Growth of English Industry and Commerce in Modern Times. The Mercantile System* (Cambridge, England, 1912), Part 3.

power. Adam Smith may well have been right about the vices of the system, but it did at least coincide with that immense commercial revolution that prepared the markets for the industrialization of Britain.

Throughout Europe the principal accomplishment of the first stage of political modernization was to build up the instrumentalities of state power on an unprecedented scale. Britain may seem backward if we think only of civilian bureaucracy. But in these combative generations of the seventeenth and eighteenth centuries the armed forces were a crucial component of the pattern of power; and with respect to her navy, British achievement was great and highly functional to her expanding commerce. Generally, the mobilization of power included and presupposed the creation of a system of taxation. In a larger sense it usually also presupposed a significant degree of economic modernization. This does not mean industrialization. As the case of Britain, economically the most advanced country, shows, the material basis of this first stage of political modernization consisted in a great expansion of trade, which was so great as to be called a "commercial revolution" but which depended typically upon cottage industry and manpower. When it came, industrialism added overwhelmingly to the forces of modernity. But in eighteenth-century Britain the modern state had sent down strong roots and shown vigorous growth long before the Industrial Revolution.

In the eighteenth century France, which, as Suzanne Berger contends,[4] had been in basic respects the first regime to modernize, began to lose its place as the model for Europe. While the Bourbons had taken the essential first steps in creating a bureaucracy, the system, judged by later standards, was still imperfectly centralized, insufficiently impersonal, and inadequately trained and specialized. Central authority could not readily control the huge body of officials, whose upper levels enjoyed hereditary tenure and titles of nobility. The fact that most offices were purchasable—the "venality" of offices—depressed standards of competence. Only later in liberal and democratic periods did the French civil service acquire its thorough-going commitment to competence in the person of the specialized *fonctionnaire*. Having, so to speak, chosen absolutism as its mode of modernization, the Bourbon monarchy proved unable to complete the indispensable next step of creating a bureaucratic instrument that would do its will. Thus, when the monarchy attempted to put its finances in order, the resistance of the nobility, entrenched in the bureaucracy, the law courts, and the provincial assemblies, precipitated the Revolution.

Yet the accomplishments of the Bourbons had been massive, one of their most critical achievements having been the creation of a system of taxation. The importance of this feature to modernity is so great that Joseph A. Schumpeter has called the modern state the "tax state" (*Steuerstaat*).

---
[4]Suzanne Berger, *The French Political System*, Chap. 1 (New York, 1974).

The financial straits of their declining days should not be allowed to obscure the immense advances the Bourbons had made over medieval fiscal methods. In France as elsewhere that meant above all moving away from an extractive system based largely on payments in kind and services. Under the feudal method of mobilizing power vassals performed military service in return for their fiefs, public works were accomplished by forced labor, officials lived off fees, and indeed the royal court found food and shelter by prolonged visits with wealthy noblemen. The establishment of a system of taxation meant that there could be a full-time paid judiciary, bureaucracy, and military and that wars and public works could be based on supplies purchased and controlled directly and fully by the central authority—all essential ingredients of modern centralization. Such an extractive system presupposed an exchange economy that would provide the money and the appropriate points of extraction. At the same time, the vast and continually growing demands of modernizing authority also promoted the growth of such an economy, as in forcing landowners to find a market for their produce in order to have the means of paying their taxes.

The work of national integration had also been carried forward under the Bourbons. Georges Lefebvre wrote:

> Toward national unity there had been indeed great progress, without which the Revolution would have been impossible. A thousand ties had been woven among Frenchmen by the development of communications and commerce, by the education given in colleges, by the attraction of the court and Paris.[5]

But local and class particularism was still strong in spite of the efforts of the monarchy. In unifying the legal system, nationalizing the market, further centralizing government, and many other ways, the Revolution of 1789 and Napoleon I achieved what the Old Regime itself had attempted.

Like France, Germany also chose the road of absolutism to modernity. As Goldman notes, this was in great part a consequence of the political disintegration resulting from the Thirty Years War. Along with the geopolitical position of Germany in the midst of potentially hostile neighbors, this meant that the military strain would be powerful in the policies and instrumentalities of the modernizing principalities, especially Prussia. There the remnants of the medieval estates were crushed by the monarchy and the energies of the nobility absorbed into the powerful bureaucracy of the eighteenth century. This system showed its capacity when the challenge of revolution came in the Napoleonic period. As Goldman observes, the Prussian bureaucracy carried through a

---

[5] Georges Lefebvre, *The Coming of the French Revolution,* R. R. Palmer (tr.) (Princeton, N. J., 1947), p. 20.

revolution from above which largely forestalled the social and political revolution which never occurred in Germany. The result was a talented and efficient, if still privileged and oligarchic, civil service, the mandarin core of the much-heralded *Beamtenstaat* and the civilian compeer of its military establishment.

In eighteenth-century Russia, to an even greater extent than in Germany, an autocratic regime with a strong modernizing thrust was established that not only barred the way to constitutionalism and representative government but also subjected all elements of society—peasantry, nobility and clergy—to the state. Not only was serfdom maintained and even strengthened, but the position of the upper classes was also far weaker than in Western Europe. "Noblemen's privileges," as Ulam writes, "were made dependent on their direct service to the state, and the nobility, as a class, was amalgamated with a bureaucratic caste."

It is necessary to dwell on these long-ago scenes if we are to understand the modern state and its tendencies and possibilities today. Democracy and liberty are, and have been for some time, under severe challenge in the West. It would be reassuring if we could find some kind of inherent support for them in the basic forces of modernity, especially in the scientific rationalism that is so sharply defined and powerful a constituent in the modern state. It would be especially helpful to know whether the dictatorial forms of the modern state in our time are inherently stable, or whether their modernity will divert them toward convergence with the liberal democratic regimes. The developments in Prussia and Russia in the eighteenth century, however, are a warning that the modern state in its autocratic form can make great strides in building up its characteristic instruments of power without suffering intolerable strains for lack of liberty.

This empirical lesson of history can be put into the general terms of power-interest dynamics. It would appear that the mobilization of power, as in the expansion of the extractive functions of the state, will strongly stimulate and support the demands and purposes pursued by means of the state. The new purposes, however, need not represent a trend toward democratization. On the contrary, the active political community may remain relatively small in numbers while its visions of national development and imperial expansion increase and multiply. The equilibrium of power and interests will be maintained, but under conditions that will hardly please the liberal democrat. Crucial questions for analysis are whether the growing capacities of the state were used for egalitarian purposes and what the role of political structure was in the determination of the choices made. In this light, the lessons of the nineteenth and twentieth centuries, while still ambiguous, are rather less gloomy. The immense mobilization of power accomplished by all European states in this time seems to show that a wider degree of participation is almost inevitable.

The Liberal Democratic Stage

If the accomplishments of the first stage had been especially marked in the mobilization of power, the emphasis in the second was on the mobilization of interests. Moreover, this increase in political scale meant not only a new order of magnitude in the scope and complexity of political demands, but also a thrust toward wider political participation. At the same time, the mobilization of power went forward. The nineteenth century saw the perfecting of a system of civil service—specialized, impersonal, hierarchical—immortalized in Max Weber's famous model. It was also the time, especially in its later decades, when the income tax spread, a mechanism of extraction that can rightly be compared with conscription. These mounting drafts on the resources of society were often major reasons why participation was extended. Also, needless to say, democratization and the efforts of ruling groups to avert it by assuaging popular needs constituted a large stimulus to the mobilization of power.

In advances toward liberal democracy the era left its mark on political history. In Britain the structure of citizenship was further elaborated by the addition of political to civil equality, mainly through the gradual and, except for a brief flare-up over women's suffrage, less and less contentious extension of the franchise. One basic condition making possible the historic advance of 1832 when the franchise was extended to the middle class was the very weakness of bureaucracy that epitomized Britain's lack of modernity. "Whig liberty" meant that the governing class was free from the menace of a royal bureaucracy or a large standing army. But it also meant that the demands for power of a burgeoning middle class could not be resisted.

Yet this rise in participation did not signify a proportionate diminution in the influence of the governing class. In great degree the middle class in the early part of this period accepted the political leadership of the upper social strata, as did the working class in turn when it received the vote and was drawn into political activity. According to a long line of observers, both foreign and domestic, the stability and progress of the British polity owe much to the survival of such traditionalist structures and sentiments.

At least the nineteenth-century British example bars the generalization that aristocratic survivals are intrinsically destabilizing—as the case of Germany may seem to imply. Indeed it will be argued in the section on Great Britain that more recent British experience further suggests not only that certain traditionalist survivals may be functional but also that a thorough-going modernity has a large potential for instability and ineffectiveness.

Britain in this period does challenge the proposition put forward earlier that the overall trend in the modern state has been toward primary centralization. It will be remembered that primary centralization is a relative growth in activity or, more precisely, an increase in the sum of the needs and resources of the members of the polity that are mobilized and related to one another by the state. While we can no longer accept the older view that for much of the nineteenth century Britain practiced a policy of strict laissez faire, it is nevertheless true that there was a sharp shift away from the intervention of the mercantilist system, involving an immense dismantling of old laws and controls. In this sense, Britain experienced a swing from collectivism to individualism.

Even though the withdrawal of control was accompanied by new sorts of intervention—for example, the first attempt to regulate factory labor in 1802—the shift in policy patterns was marked. The three sets of figures in Table 7.1 give rough indications of what happened.

Table 7.1 Government Expenditure (1900 prices)

	Total Expenditure (in Millions of Pounds Sterling)	Per Capita Expenditure (in Millions of Pounds Sterling)	Total Expenditure (as percentage of G.N.P.)
1792	17	1.2	11
1822	49	2.3	19
1850	62	2.3	12
1900	268	6.5	15
1938	851	17.9	30.1
1955	1,309	25.7	37.3

DATA SOURCE: Alan T. Peacock and Jack Wiseman, *The Growth of Public Expenditure in the United Kingdom* (Princeton, N. J.: Princeton University Press, 1961), Tables 1 and 2.

The first column reflects the steady expansion of state activity from the late eighteenth to the mid-twentieth century. The sums are in constant prices and so show a relatively greater sum of resources being taken and used by the state from one point in time to the next. The second column, which measures per capita expenditure, brings out the impact of laissez faire. Conventionally, historians have said that there was a period of reduced governmental intervention in the second quarter of the nineteenth century. The table shows not a reduced, but at any rate a constant level of per capita expenditure. The third column, which sets forth total governmental expenditure in comparison with GNP, suggests a later major change in policy pattern. As industrialization moved forward after the Napoleonic Wars, governmental expenditure, even though rising, took an ever lower portion of the national product. This trend, however, was reversed toward the end of the century, the change coming between 1890 and 1900. During the interwar years the index mounted sharply. It is in these decades that the rise of the welfare state and what I have called the collectivist stage of modernization are usually placed.

Looked at in a broad perspective, the pattern of development in France was very much the same as that in Britain. This must be emphasized, because comparisons of the two countries are usually employed to display contrasts and dissimilarities. That is a useful way of bringing out their more subtle features, precisely because in the context of European, not to mention world, politics, Britain and France are and long have been very much alike. During the nineteenth century the French bureaucracy was perfected; patronage was finally eliminated and professional training built into the system to create the *fonctionnaire*. The franchise was extended to the point of universal male suffrage, although not with the majestic gradualism of the British experience. Industrial capitalism arose, although later than in Britain and leaving a larger agrarian sector of peasant owners. By 1914 France, like Britain, was a powerful, democratic, industrialized state that had achieved a level of national integration comparable to its power and prosperity. The proof came when it sustained the staggering losses of World War I—1.4 million military deaths—yet fought on for four years without serious internal dissent.

The differences between Britain and France at this time hinge mainly on certain peculiarities of the French Revolution, the event that inaugurated the French transition to the liberal democratic age. It was a highly self-conscious, modernizing revolution. Reason, science, democracy, secularism, and national progress were proclaimed and pursued by its leaders with fanatical commitment. In the language of the revolutionaries, France was only then breaking out of the Middle Ages. In fact, as we have seen, the French monarchy had long since accomplished that transition; the significance of the revolutionary period was that it moved France not into modernity but from the early to the middle period of modernization. In this sense, its function was similar to that of the great British reforms of the early nineteenth century. Accurate or not, the revolutionary claims were made with a grand style that gave an indelible character to a wide spectrum of French political behavior. From the calling of the Estates General to Waterloo, the drama of men and factions created a repertory of role models to which the French revert with what amounts to repetition compulsion—consider the events of May 1968, for example. The term may not be clinically exact, but it brings out the fact that in the development of the polity, as of the individual, the choices made and attempted at crucial moments of decision can determine a whole pattern of typical behavior for generations to come. As a result, whenever there is renewed crisis and confusion, men revert to these old designs of response, especially when the originals were executed with the superb aesthetic power of the great revolutionary and Napoleonic figures. In the nineteenth century, let the tocsin sound however faintly, and instantly countless French hearts acknowledged the nation's call for a new Robespierre, Saint-Just, Danton, and, not least, Napoleon.

The result of this peculiar past is that, as Suzanne Berger writes, French politics represents "the tradition of modernity." Since the revolutionary period, there has always been available in the past a detailed model for any modernizing regime. Curiously, therefore, French progressives, while trying to construct the future, have looked backward for guidance. This has imparted not only the atmosphere of traditionalism to their behavior, but also its rigidities. The central conflict over legitimacy in French political culture, for example, turns on the clash of presidential and parliamentary regimes, the strong executive versus the representative legislature. These two can be reconciled, as the British experience shows. But French reactions have long been fixed by the template of historical memory that opposes the *regime conventionnel* of the Revolution of 1789 to the Bourbon or Napoleonic executive. As any tourist knows, the political graffiti on Parisian walls cannot be appreciated without a knowledge of what Berger calls "political archaeology." These slogans still proclaim not only *"La commune vaincra"*—after all that was only one hundred years ago—but also *"Vive le roi."*

The German experience may not appear to fit under the title of liberal democratic stage that I have given to this second phase of modernization. In Germany liberal democracy did not rise and unfold increment by increment, as in Britain, nor by spasmodic advance and retreat, as in France. Although industrialism came with a mighty rush in the second half of the nineteenth century, these years only underline the lesson that capitalism does not necessarily or effortlessly bring liberalism and democracy. That this correlation can be found in British and French history does not make it any more natural than the correlation of capitalism with authoritarian government in Prussia—not to mention Russia. The essence of this stage of German political development, as Goldman brings out, is that a bureaucratic-aristocratic regime continued to be sufficiently adaptable to maintain the privileged position of its landowning and military elites and to assure their dominance in an alliance with the new industrial and commercial classes. Moreover, the regime had the power—if necessary the armed force—to crush any thrust for power by liberals or democrats, as in 1848. The contrast with Britain in this respect shows the importance there of "Whig liberty" for peaceful parliamentary reform and for the entrance of the middle class into the active political community. If in 1832 the Duke of Wellington had commanded a large standing army and a centralized bureaucracy on the Prussian model, it is hard not to believe that he would have suppressed the demand for the reform bill instead of winning the Lords' acquiescence to it.

The German bourgeoisie, as Goldman shows, were reconciled with an authoritarian state and a conservative social order. Indeed, they lent their support to the suppression and restraint of those very freedoms with which they were identified in Britain and France. From this alliance the capitalist classes reaped substantial material advantages; as German national unity was achieved under Prussian hegemony, they benefited from the usual opportunities for modernization that arise from a wide national market. The state also supported a massive system of external protection and internal subvention, including public construction and ownership of railroads. From such measures German capitalism acquired a special character contrasting with the capitalism of Britain.

These peculiarities were further developed by the advanced policy of social security carried out in the latter part of the nineteenth century. While the socialist and trade-union movement nonetheless continued to grow, it cannot be denied that the working class, like the middle class before it, was in significant measure reconciled to the established order. In Germany, as in France, the socialists in the legislature voted war credits in 1914. Indeed, considering how deeply the problem of national identity had perplexed Germany for most of the nineteenth century, the population as a whole during World War I showed a solidarity remarkably high and in no way inferior to that of Britain and France—in four years the military deaths were 1.8 million. Only toward the end, when confronted by defeat, did the system begin to crack.

As Goldman shows, the peculiarities of modernization in Germany's liberal democratic era prepared the way for the fatal weaknesses of Weimar. Yet it is crucial not to be preoccupied with the causes of that tragic episode of German political development. The imperial system between 1871 and 1914 was in many respects progressive and promising. While it was a *Beamtenstaat* (bureaucratic state), it was also a *Rechstsstaat* (rule-of-law state), in which a highly trained bureaucracy and judiciary gave the country an administration of the law that was impartial and incorruptible. Likewise, the regime moved toward a more popular government—after 1871 the lower house of the imperial legislature was elected by universal manhood suffrage, although to be sure the effect of this provision was more than overbalanced by the predominance of conservative Prussia in the whole scheme. Under the Weimar Republic a liberal democratic constitution was adopted. In spite of its failings, the politics of this regime were open and responsive—by no means doomed from the start to collapse in fascism.

Ulam remarks that in the nineteenth century "Russia stood as the fortress of militarism and national and social oppression, a seeming exception to all the rules of historical development as propounded by liberalism."[6] In the previous century its modernizing monarchs, like other enlightened

---

[6] Adam B. Ulam, *The Russian Political System*, Chap. 1 (New York, 1974).

despots, had sought to improve education and raise bureaucratic efficiency. In the course of time, science took root and flourished; progress in such subjects as celestial mechanics, for instance, laid the groundwork for the later Soviet achievements in space. Although coming late to industrial development, once Russia entered the industrial race, its rate of growth compared favorably with that of advanced countries. During the last decade of the nineteenth century Russian increases in the production of iron and coal exceeded those of Britain, Germany, or the United States. Yet in spite of these undoubted advances in political, economic, and cultural modernization, the Russian polity showed only the faintest traces of movement toward liberalism and democracy.

Indeed, it is a question whether the economy itself could properly be called capitalist. Capitalism requires a free market in labor as in goods, but the great bulk of the Russian work force was held in serfdom until 1861. Even thereafter, as Ulam shows, the powers of the *mir,* the village organization, were not only anti-industrial, but anticapitalist in spirit and effect. Generally, the extensive system of governmental intervention established in the days of Peter the Great survived strongly in the nineteenth century, when the countries of Western Europe were throwing off the collectivist restraints of mercantilism. While industrialism finally did take hold and thrive, the mode of production was capitalistic in an even more qualified sense than that of Prussia, because the government exercised a critical directing role in industrialization. The Russian experience again reinforces the hypothesis that modernization is compatible with a highly authoritarian regime.

Yet the Russian case also suggests that the power and efficiency that modernity brings can only be partially realized by an old-fashioned autocracy. As measured by at least three of the indexes of political modernity —power, participation, and national integration—Russia on the eve of World War I lagged far behind the other three polities. The war confirmed these indications, revealing incredible inefficiency in the bureaucracy and armed forces, as a series of terrible defeats, in which military deaths ran to 1.7 million, undermined popular support for the regime and precipitated revolution.

The tsars had learned only too well how to restrain and control political mobilization. During the nineteenth century, although the regime showed little movement toward liberal democracy, the pressures were there. The doctrines of the French Revolution spread to Russia and, despite the fierce repressions of the tsarist police-state, deeply affected small groups of the upper classes, especially the intellectuals. These doctrines inspired a long series of efforts toward achieving liberation. The regime did not respond either by granting a modicum of real power, as happened in Britain and France, or by conceding material advantages, as in Germany. Of course, it could not have conceived of the Soviet solution of participation without power. When the years before the revolution led to some movement toward constitutional monarchy, the steps were small and faltering. Although economic modernization does not necessarily imply liberal democracy, it seems clear that the mobilization of power in the modern state requires a commensurate mobilization of interests of some sort. In this sense the inability of the regime to modernize its instrumentalities of power derived from its failure to modernize its politics.

The Collectivist Stage

With due allowance for profound national differences, the previous pages have sketched the common course of modernization. The focus has been dual. One theme has been the linear trends toward greater power, scale, interdependence, and centralization that prevailed through all stages. Another theme has been the qualitative changes in regime for each stage—the distinctive configurations of policy, the new forms of bureaucracy, and the shifts in the constellation of governing classes and intellectual elites. Since the form and fortunes of the four polities during the third stage of modernization is the subject matter of the principal sections of this book, it is not appropriate to continue this country-by-country sketch. A few general propositions will be offered, however, about how these regimes achieved their present common structure and what common problems are inherent in it.

When we ask how and why states changed from nineteenth-century liberalism to the age of the welfare state and planned economy, one plausible approach is to start with the development of the economy. When discussing economic modernization at an earlier point, I observed that in the British case the modern era in economic development can be divided into the periods of the commercial revolution, industrial revolution, and organizational revolution. By the last category I mean especially the rise of the modern corporation to a place of dominance in economy, but also the spread of large-scale organization in such forms as employers associations, trade unions, farmers and peasants groups, and professional associations. Under such influences, it is often argued, the market economy of the old classical economies declined and ceased to perform its function of efficiently allocating resources among various uses and rewards among various factors of production. Slumps and stagnation resulted within nations and in the world economy, forcing governments to intervene more and more drastically to supplement and supersede the automatic working of the market.

Such an interpretation is not implausible when applied to the British experience. If we take the longer and wider view imposed by modernization theory, however, the greater importance of political factors appears.

Even in individualist thought the national purpose of economic development was well understood and highly valued. Adam Smith made his central concern the problem of how to heighten the annual increase in the wealth of nations. Also, as the practice of the continental countries shows, some governments intervened extensively even in the heyday of economic liberalism. To recur again to an observation of Charles Tilly, when capitalism arose, it did not come into existence as a "natural force" independent of state policy but, on the contrary, had to be encouraged, promoted, and often forcibly imposed by comprehensive state action. The liberal economic order, in short, was in great degree a creature of public policy—which might well be expected to change in fundamentals again in the course of political development.

Such a shift in fundamentals took place, especially with the rise of working-class politics, in the latter part of the nineteenth century. Most strikingly this new factor took form in the emergence of socialist parties, but it also had its impact on the liberal parties and, indeed, as the German and British cases show, upon conservative sectors. That powerful thrust of the modern spirit for equality that had been expressed in guarantees of legal rights and political rights now found expression in the demand for social rights. The formulation of these demands came overwhelmingly from reformist and radical intellectuals. The electoral—and physical—force to support them derived from the newly enfranchised and recently urbanized working class.

The beginnings of the welfare state go back to a time when the capitalist economy was at its prime and the standard of living of the working class was rising. Viewed from this perspective, the planned economy was an accidental offshoot of the welfare state. To put the matter very simply: As the state developed massive programs of expenditure, it was inevitable that its actions would profoundly affect the economy and only logical that it should attempt to calculate and control these effects.

Still another source of state intervention that springs from the deeper undercurrents of modernity is the development of problem-solving knowledge and skills. This development has gone on constantly during modern times. In the liberal democratic era, for instance, the policy of "sanitation," which constituted an obvious and major departure from laissez faire, was vastly stimulated and in many respects made possible by advances in scientific knowledge—particularly in the emergence of the science of bacteriology, with all that it implied for control of disease. Perhaps the major example of the transforming effect of knowledge on public policy was the impact of Keynesian economics. This new knowledge of economic process gave direction to the huge expenditures of the welfare state; it also did much to legitimize them.

The key processes in the transition to this third stage are to be found not so much in the interrelations of economy and polity as in the internal processes of the polity, especially in what I have called the power-interest dynamic. Generally in Western Europe, the rising tide of democratic demands worked with the growing scope of scientific possibility to create the massive structures of the collectivist pattern of policy. This interrelationship can be observed even in Russia. It does not apply to the Revolution, when in the name of equality a new and far more effective modernizing elite was put in power. Once the task of industrialization had been accomplished in the time-honored Russian manner, however, the pressures for higher material well-being and even for "liberalization" began to assert themselves. Although Russia has been at the autocratic extreme throughout the modern period, some observers profess to see in these pressures some signs of convergence with attitudes in the democratic welfare states of Western Europe.

The forces that led to these changes in the pattern of policy also transformed power structure and politics. Political parties have an intrinsic connection with modernization. They presuppose and grow out of large-scale law making, the legitimacy of opposition, and organized and continuous political combat. Parties can be found in all stages of modernity, but, like the bureaucracy, they take different forms, depending upon the values and structure of the prevailing regime. The collectivist age typically brings forth the programmatic mass party. Both adjectives are exaggerations, but they serve to mark radical changes in form and process from the parties based on small cadres and broad principles that prevailed before the arrival of universal suffrage. The new socialist parties are usually the innovators, but older parties have known how to adapt.

In this time of transition, class and class interests have become much more explicitly the center of political controversy. The philosophy and rhetoric of this new definition of the political situation derived from powerful intellectual elites, of which the various Marxist schools were the more influential. As a result, the political demands of substantial parts of the working-class electorates of different countries were shaped by socialist doctrine, and class membership became an important determinant of political behavior and party allegiance. As we shall see in the discussions of the various party systems, however, class never became more than one among several determinants. The correlation is closest in Britain, where other bases of party allegiance, such as religion and nationality, are weak. In Germany these other factors have cut across class divisions, as in religious groupings, such as the Zentrum party of Weimar, or in the persisting force of Bavarian regionalism.

In France class analysis breaks down completely as an explanation of party allegiance. In a striking tabulation Berger shows that occupation and economic status display almost no correlation with French party affiliation; parties of the Left have much the same class profile as parties of the Right. The main formative influence in France has been the conflict of Church and state. This conflict, which culminated in the late nineteenth century at the time that large-scale political parties were first being formed, has not only continued to serve as the principal axis of division between Left and Right, but also to color the whole of French politics with the high ideological fervor of a struggle over ultimate values. In Britain, on the other hand, where class division has been strongest, the issues, having been seen as essentially economic and quantitative, have been handled in a spirit of compromise and practical reform.

While there have been common trends in the patterns of participation, the national differences have remained strong. The French party system, with its multiplicity, indiscipline, and ideological overtones, contrasts with the British system, with its dualism, high cohesion, and sturdy pragmatism. With regard to the bureaucratic element of the collectivist state, however, the common traits are far more marked. The Weberian model is not a bad approximation of the common ideal. The emergence of the managed economy has added to this model a strong element of corporatism, as the powerful producers organizations of the contemporary economy have been drawn into close relationships with the formal agents of the state. Generally, also, the advance of science and the greater complexity of public policy have given the bureaucratic expert ever greater influence.

Such similarities in bureaucratic structures reflect the tendency of science to have a uniform impact. Moreover, the bureaucracy is in the realm of instrumentalities and is therefore more flexible and responsive to modernization. Parties, on the other hand, are more deeply involved in the world of expressive symbolism and consummatory values. Like the formal machinery of government in which they are embedded, they are strongly colored by national character and national history. For example, Berger finds that French parties can be best understood by a kind of political "archaeology," which reveals the historical roots of their parochialism and resistance to change. In general, national differences, whether deriving from a premodern heritage or from peculiarities of national development, have managed to survive strongly even in the present era of the highly developed modern polity.

Eight

Problems of the Developed Modern Polity

The previous pages have shown how a complex of common influences affects all countries, and not trivially but in sufficient degree to justify speaking of the modern state as a distinctive type of polity. Among other things this means that its common features produce similar patterns of consequences, which appear as problems to members of these states.

National differences affect these patterns of consequences. So, for instance, the ancient autocratic tradition of Russia greatly enhances the authoritarian tendencies of industrialism and bureaucracy. Yet these tendencies are inherent in the political and economic features of modernity and in some degree also appear in the other three modern societies. Similarly, certain peculiarities of German political culture and structure weakened the resistance of Weimar democracy to the demagogic mass politics of the Nazis. Yet the impact of modernization elsewhere has also created the political weaknesses that lead to fascist movements, even though these movements have been able to seize power in only a few cases. A principal virtue of carrying on comparative study with the aid of modernization theory is that its concepts help us see the sources of such tendencies and eventualities, which otherwise might be overlooked if national traits alone were considered responsible. The disorders of modernity afflict all advanced countries, but in different degrees.

The Problem of Effectiveness

The problems of the highly developed modern polity may conveniently be considered under two headings: the problem of effectiveness and the problem of authority. The first centers on the question of performance: To what extent does a state achieve the ends pursued through it? How well does it bear its "load" of problem solving? It may seem paradoxical that effectiveness is presented as a primary problem of the modern state, since it is in this sphere of performance and power that political modernity has scored its most distinctive successes. Yet the very order that is responsible for these successes also intrinsically gives rise to counterproductive tendencies. It has the vices of its virtues. Modernization has endowed the instrumentalities of the state with unprecedented power over man and nature. At the same time, because of their size and complexity, it is exceedingly hard to subject these instrumentalities to coherent, overall control. They continually threaten to break loose from the purposes of public policy and to drag along the whole polity on a chaotic and unintended course.

It is supremely ironic, not to say dangerous, that these powerful agencies, with their great potential for gratifying human wishes, should also be so prone to frustrate them. In the days of laissez faire in the nineteenth century, men rightly feared the unregulated economy as the source of coercive social forces. Today the polity, including the very instruments designed to modify and control the economic environment, has joined and in some countries superseded the economy as the machine that threatens to master man. Bureaucratization matches industrialization as a source of blind development. Every modern state is confronted with an unending struggle to subject to control its agencies of control. The first problem of a highly developed modern state is to master its own inordinate power.

When speaking of the state machine threatening to master man, I refer not to the problem of tyranny or other intentional abuse of authority but to the problem of control. This prospect threatens dictatorial regimes as well as liberal democracies. The menace of *accidental* nuclear war hangs over both sorts of polity. Less terrifying, but more typical of the problem, are the latent dysfunctions that burden, disrupt, and distort the huge bureaucratic machines of the modern state.

The public sector in Russia is virtually all-encompassing: Every factory and every store is owned and run by the state, and every acre of land is under its control. Adam B. Ulam describes and analyzes the difficulty of making the controls over this huge public sector respond to the will of the Communist elite.[1] He traces, for instance, the cycle of centralization-

---
[1] Adam B. Ulam, *The Russian Political System*, Chap. 4 (New York, 1974).

decentralization-recentralization produced by the forces of Soviet bureaucracy. There are special qualities in this process deriving from the nature of the dictatorship. But the process also displays a dynamic that will be familiar to students of administration in the democratic countries. Overcentralization, needless to say, plagues the command economy of the Soviet regime as well as the democratic welfare state. In Russia as elsewhere, to make savings in personnel, to avoid wasteful duplication, and to give greater initiative to people on the spot are standard reasons for reforms of administrative decentralization. So also is recentralization a familiar consequence in modern regimes, democratic or dictatorial, when the decentralized structure works to put local interests ahead of what the central decision makers regard as the national interest.

Incoherence and Incompetence

To say that there is a problem in subjecting the vast complex of power mobilized by the modern state to coherent control implies that an effort is being made to assert such control and that there is some more or less unified will or scheme of priorities issuing from the politics of the system. This assumption is legitimate as a device for isolating and identifying tendencies inherent in the modern pattern of power. It brings out the fact that incoherence in the pattern of policy may proceed from such objective forces and need not be referred back to some conflict or disorientation in the directing will of the state. In practice, of course, the directing will of the state is itself often the source of chaos and ineffectiveness. The tendency of the pattern of interests to produce incoherent decision making is a major and common problem of the modern polity.

The terms coherence and incoherence do not have the connotation of deep seriousness. Yet, fragmentation in the polity and incoherence in the policy-making process have led to some of the more profound and characteristic failures of the highly developed modern state. The most tragic case was the fall of the Weimar Republic. Under this system, based on the best models of liberal, democratic constitutionalism, the public will splintered into a multitude of political parties, which were represented in the legislature with meticulous accuracy and fairness through a proportional system. In consequence, as Guido Goldman shows, no single party was ever strong enough to form a majority government, and Cabinets, being necessarily based on multiparty support, were short-lived and often paralyzed by internal disagreement.[2] The resulting lack of governance, which the Germans strikingly referred to as "pluralistic stagnation" *(pluralistische Stockung),* greatly promoted the economic and political disorder that discred-

---

[2] Guido Goldman, *The German Political System*, Chap. 2 (New York, 1974).

ited self-government and strengthened the appeal of the authoritarian extremists.

Nor have the dire results of democratic pluralism been confined to Germany. The multiparty system of France had similar, although not such tragic, effects on the policy making of the Third and Fourth Republics. *Immobilisme* was a characteristic failing of governments under these constitutions. Charles deGaulle made it a principal object of denunciation in his attack upon the "regime of parties." As Suzanne Berger points out, the new constitutional and political regime of 1958 represented an attempt of the French polity to shake off this typical weakness of multiparty democracy.[3] Moreover, two-party democracy itself is by no means free of the basic flaw. A majority party may perform its conventional function of "aggregating interests," yet in the course of this process commit itself to compromises and respond to pressures to such an extent that its policies are as short-sighted and conflicting as those of a multiparty coalition. In Britain, the home of party dualism and strong Cabinet government, the power of pressure groups in recent years has been a major reason for the inflationary tendencies that have done much to frustrate a policy of sustained economic growth. The system of collectivist politics, which became stabilized in the fifties, was based not only on a consensus among the main political groups, but also upon a balance of pressures that severely limited the scope of decisive action.

Modernization promotes pluralism through its characteristic process of division of labor. The disruptive tendencies of that result are further enhanced by the egalitarian thrust of modernity. The basic doctrines of egalitarianism—that every man is the best judge of his own interest and that all men are the best judge of the common interest—brush aside the claims of traditional governing classes and of professionally trained elites. The resulting demands on the part of voters for plausible rhetoric and immediate gratifications can only further diminish the effectiveness of public policy.

In the face of these familiar vices of modern democracy, it is not absurd to suggest that an authoritarian system, as in Soviet Russia, is more functional to the needs of the modern polity, at any rate in its more advanced stages. Given the inevitable complexities of policy and the inevitable pluralism of social strata in these later stages, it would seem prudent to entrust the democratic electorate with only a restricted role in the governmental process. From a general view, it appears that a mature industrialism tends strongly toward a hierarchical form of organization. Trade unions do arise and acquire powers of collective bargaining in free countries. Yet the

---

[3]Suzanne Berger, *The French Political System*, Chap. 2 (New York, 1974).

prerogatives of management are maintained and the typical firm or corporation is run from the top, not from the shop floor or by the shareholders. This being so, it would seem logical to believe that the hierarchical form would also be more suitable for the governance of the economy as a whole. Such a government would tend to reduce the distorting and frustrating pressures with which a free society obstructs the orderly and effective conduct of affairs. An authoritarian regime would presumably have a better chance of ensuring that a unified and professional outlook would prevail among the decision makers.

The experience of Russia, which was burdened by a rigidly autocratic tradition, a particularly dogmatic version of Marxism, and a large traditional sector in its economy, may not be a fair test of this hypothesis. But even after making allowance for these special national circumstances, the implications of the Russian experience are that the authoritarian version of the modern polity also has its own deep-seated dysfunctions. The question is not the liberty or humanity of such a regime. The case for this sort of regime is precisely that these values are sacrificed for the sake of a higher achievement according to that other criterion of modernity, effective performance—that is, in terms of this analysis, the power of the state over the social and natural environment.

Now if we pass over for the time being the question of whether the Soviet regime meets the two requisites of effectiveness already mentioned (*coherence* and *professional competence*), it is still clear from Ulam's account that it confronts serious problems in meeting two other requisites, the need for *criticism* and the need for *active cooperation and consent* among the governed. As Ulam observes, an authoritarian system of administration promotes efficiency, but "only up to a certain point." If any complex system of action is effectively to pursue its goals, there must be provision for a constant feedback of informed criticism into the decision-making process. In a liberal regime, a major function of its liberal institutions is to make possible a flow of reports, criticism, and counterproposals from within the bureaucracy and from the society at large. By many means, formal and informal, from the press, parties, pressure groups, legislative committees, and systems of administrative oversight, messages get through—admittedly confused by an immense amount of static—regarding the empirical relevance and technical appropriateness of governmental action. To governments these messages may be "thorns of criticism," to use Otto von Bismarck's words. Yet, as he himself recognized when he coined the phrase in his later years, they are indispensable in the long run to effective performance.

That further requisite, the need to mobilize consent among the governed, becomes ever more critical as the scope of policy grows. The process of primary centralization means that government touches more and more people in more and more ways. Among the democratic regimes, contemporary governments impose large and growing burdens upon their citizens, not only in the form of deprivations of money, time, effort, and so on—as in the payment of taxes or the performance of military service—but, even more important in these days of the welfare state and managed economy, in requiring intricate patterns of behavior—such as conformity to wage and price "guidelines." In Russia this immediate impact is multiplied by the far wider responsibilities of the regime. For either type of polity, as the scope of government action grows, sheer coercion is less and less adequate as a base of obedience. In countless ways, not mere conformity to orders but willing cooperation expressing intelligent understanding is necessary if the modern state is to achieve its goals.

Traditionally, one major means of mobilizing the consent needed by the modernizing state has been to extend the circle of participation. One function of the democratization of the polity in Western Europe has been to win consent, support, and cooperation for its growing activities. The extension of the franchise has paralleled the progress of primary centralization. Similarly, the rise of functional representation, which has brought organized producers groups from business, labor, and agriculture into close consultation with governmental departments, has been in great part impelled by the need of governments to have the advice and cooperation of the leaders and members of these groups.

Having foregone the means of performing these functions that are provided by liberal democracy, the Soviet regime has attempted to find substitutes suitable to its form of rule. For example, the congress of representatives of collective farms held in 1969 had as its purpose to boost the morale of the collective peasant and to emphasize the importance of that branch of the agrarian economy. Broadly speaking, the main instrument for performing both the function of watching over and checking the bureaucracy and the function of arousing and maintaining support among the populace for the regime has been the Communist party. Its presence and functioning justify referring to the Soviet regime as "partisan and participatory." In the liberal democracies also political parties provide criticism and help win support for the regime by giving the governed a sense of participation. The single party of the Soviet Union, however, performs these functions in a totally different manner, reflecting the will of the Communist elite rather than the purposes and interests of a democratic electorate.

It would seem that any modern authoritarian regime must find it necessary to have such a party apparatus to carry out functions indispensable to the effective performance of the polity. But the commitment to a one-party system itself entails further consequences that are severely dysfunctional. Such parties are usually highly ideological, and probably could not perform their task of mobilizing consent unless they were. Yet an ideological commitment hampers flexibility and adaptation and may embody conceptions of empirical reality that conflict with scientific advance. The grotesque and wasteful results of Lysenkoism in Russia illustrate the dangers. Moreover, although the pluralism of the democratic electorate is repressed by "democratic centralism," conflicts within a small ruling elite can be even more intense and destructive. For this reason, in an authoritarian system there may be, even in a collegial regime (that is, a regime in which supreme authority is shared by a body of colleagues), a tendency toward one-man rule—a kind of Hobbesian logic leading to an absolute sovereign. Yet the irrationalities of autocracy, whether Stalin's paranoia or Khrushchev's "hare-brained schemes," are highly dysfunctional to the purposes of modernity. While liberty and democracy are less needed by modernity than was once supposed and while there is no reason to expect an inevitable liberalization of the Soviet regime, Soviet authoritarianism, as Ulam's account demonstrates, creates tensions and contradictions that could lead to major disruption.

The effectiveness of modern democracies is threatened by inherent tendencies toward incoherence of the public will and incompetence in the ruling powers. Yet the authoritarian alternative also suffers from severe deficiencies at both levels of the political process. The public will may be unified in a degree beyond the reach of pluralistic democracy, but the means by which this unity is achieved tend to create rigidities that are at least as counterproductive as the immobilism that may afflict popular government. Moreover, while unchecked authority nominally creates the opportunity to put the highest professional competence in command of the instruments of state power, the same structure impairs the adaptive and responsive capacities of the system at every level. Democratic incoherence and incompetence are matched by the rigidities and irrelevancy of authoritarian systems.

No doubt the most serious question of all is whether terror is inherent in modern authoritarianism. The destructiveness and dysfunctionality of terror are plain from the record of tragic and colossal blunders of Stalinism, ranging from collectivization to the "permanent purge." The notion of a single and incontestable truth that is embodied in the ideological one-party system makes the toleration of honest differences of opinion virtually impossible. Every critic and every dissident must appear to authority as a traitor and plotter. But given the complexity and fluidity of modern social change, differences of opinion are bound to arise. The effort to repress them and prevent them will therefore follow. In this sense, Stalinism was inherent in Leninism.

The Problem of Authority

The other major problem afflicting the developed modern state is the problem of authority. Any polity confronts the task of legitimizing the exercise of power by its rulers. But a special problem of authority afflicts political modernity, going back to its very beginnings. This problem arises from the fact that the basic attitudes of modernity, rationalism and voluntarism, mount a harsh and powerful attack upon the foundations of traditional authority, while themselves providing only vulnerable substitutes. The regimes produced by medieval political development had been sustained by doctrines grounded in a universal religious faith and by sentiments engendered by ancient communities founded on locality and lordship. The "acids of modernity" deeply eroded these foundations of legitimacy. The secularization of the state, whether or not there was outright separation of church and state or disestablishment of the church, deprived it of explicit ecclesiastical support. More seriously, the scientific and rationalistic attacks on religion weakened its old doctrines of civil order, which had justified as well as defined and limited the role of the polity. At the same time, the old bonds of communal attachment were worn away both by the new values celebrating contractual association and by the vast mobility of a modernizing society.

In place of these older grounds of political obligation, modern thought offers characteristic substitutes. In keeping with the nature of modernity, these can be neither transcendental nor traditional, but are contractual and ideological. In the first place, the state is sharply seen as an instrument of benefits to its members, in return for which they contribute support. Over time the content of the benefits has changed, from mere law and order and defense to the goods and services of the welfare state, as have the material embodiments of support, such as taxes, military service, and cooperation with the managed economy. Yet in practice, as in theory, the transaction remains essentially economic, a kind of mass purchase by citizens from the state of things they could not conveniently get through the market and individual action. As an economic transaction, moreover, the delivery of support depends upon the purchasers continuing to feel that they are getting full value for their contribution. Intrinsically, therefore, like customers in the market, they are free to withdraw support when their expectations are not fulfilled. Such attitudes put great emphasis upon the output efficiency of the modern state, a responsibility which, given the modern stress on high instrumental performance, the modern state has vigorously sought to meet. The economic and rationalist character of the relationship, however, has made the acceptance of modern authority precarious in contrast with the acceptance of forms and persons in traditional societies.

Ideologies constitute the second characteristic means by which modern states seek legitimacy. Three centuries of modernity have produced a dazzling variety of them in contrast to the massive uniformity of opinion that, apart from the conflict of *imperium* and *sacerdotium,* marked the previous thousand years. The conflict of "isms," which is typical of and indeed unique to modern times, has given rise to continual controversy over conceptions of authority and common purpose and to frequent efforts to change regimes. As systems of thought and ideals, ideologies have had and continue to have enormous influence. On the other hand, so long as they merely express intellectual belief and moral conviction, they fail to draw on the other strong grounds of motivation inhering in habit, emotion, and identification that supported traditional solidary groups. Like the bonds of contract, the bonds of ideology depend heavily upon conscious, rational processes, and so they suffer from a certain fragility.

These limitations of contract and ideology give rise to the classic problem of authority in the modern state. The course of modern political development provides abundant illustrations of this problem. The historical record, however, also shows that the authority and cohesion of the polity have been strongly supplemented by other supports. First is the fact of nationality. Deriving from premodern sources, nationality has provided a focus of identification, engaging deep-seated affectual energies and supporting a kind of solidarity similar to that in traditional communities. The modern states that have survived have been nation-states.

We need not dwell here on nationality, as its role has been given a good deal of attention in previous pages. A second source of support, which needs more attention, is economic class. Although usually thought of as a source of division and conflict, economic class must also be seen as a major instrument in maintaining the cohesion of the polity: In modern political development it functions as a source of stability as well as of movement. As a stabilizing factor, economic class has a twofold effect. In the first place, a sense of class is a powerful aggregating influence. Nowadays, the division of labor multiplies almost indefinitely the occupational groupings within the working force. In turn, these groupings form the basis for much of the organization of the pressure-group sector of the pattern of interests. Economic class, however, transcends these groupings, constituting a basis for concerted action among a wide portion of the electorate. In Britain, for instance, the strong dualism of class identity among voters has been one of the principal bases for the two-party system. The aggregating function of this factor can be seen by comparison with countries, such as the United States, where a weaker sense of class identity coincides with far less solidary party behavior.

Moreover, not only does class help suppress the pluralism of the modern mass electorate, but when attached to a political party, it also enhances the voters' sense of efficacy. In the huge electorates of present-day democracies, it is hard for the individual to see his participation as having influence on the polity. Indeed, where such large numbers are involved, the act of voting is so insignificant as to make little sense from the point of view of the lone individual. But while individuals cannot win elections, a class can. The voter who identifies with a class and its party can have feelings of victory, power, and self-government when this party wins elections or in other ways influences the state. In this way class can strengthen the familiar device of participation as a means of creating support for the modern polity.

Class can perform this function of aggregating economic interests because it is not itself solely an economic phenomenon. As the case of the United States shows, merely having a highly developed industrial economy is a necessary but not sufficient condition for a strong sense of class and a high level of class cohesion in political behavior. The latter types of behavior, as seen in European countries, depend also upon a political culture that still bears the marks of its origins in the hierarchical, corporate society of premodern times. As I argue in my discussion of class and politics in Britain, a "sense of degree" deriving from such a political culture prepares the perceptions of the British voter, making him more liable to find social stratification and to identify with a class.

The New Fragmentation

In general, the problem of authority is solved to the degree that the commands of government and the behavior of citizens coincide. Such coincidence will depend upon two variables: the burdens imposed upon citizens and their grounds for compliance. There is reason to believe that certain conditions created by the later stages of modernization make this equilibrium much harder to achieve than it was in earlier stages, and so raise the problem of authority to a new plane of intensity. With regard to burdens, it takes no prolonged argument to show that their weight is vastly increased in the era of collectivist policy. This is a period of growing intervention by the state, which progressively extends its regulatory and extractive activities. One rough indicator of the trend is the increase in taxation, not only absolutely but also as a percentage of the national income. There are complex questions of the changing incidence of these burdens. Yet it seems highly likely that, for comparable individuals or groups, the gross burden of state action has increased immensely in the course of the past two generations in the countries of Western Europe.

The further question of net burden and of the perception of that burden turn attention to the other side of the equation, the grounds of compliance. It is with regard to this variable that the most complex and subtle transformations have been taking place. On balance it would seem that both the rational and nonrational grounds for compliance have been weakening. Initially, at any rate, as Gunnar Myrdal has observed (see Chapter 5), the welfare state with its panoply of benefits surely heightened political integration. On the other hand, the connection between burdens and benefits has been obscured by the inherently complex and technical modes of action of the modern polity. Budgets for five years or so have become common; a government can hardly launch, let alone complete, a major program or change of program within the old annual cycle. Furthermore, the technical aspects of problems and programs—for example the economics of inflation—are so difficult as to defeat all but professionally trained minds. All this makes it hard for the individual to connect burden and benefit, to see the immediate sacrifice as a necessary cost of the ultimate outcome. Whether he values that outcome as a quid pro quo for himself or as a fulfillment of his ideals, the loss of rationale diminishes his willingness to tolerate the readily perceivable and relentlessly mounting costs.

The essential point is familiar to historians of democratic theory. The plausibility of that idea as the foundation of a viable polity depended not only upon an explicit belief in the rational competence of the voter but also upon an implicit assumption that the operations of government would remain comprehensible. We may think highly of the common man and yet conclude that modern government transcends his comprehension and patience.

Characteristic processes of modernization are also eroding the nonrational grounds. The most interesting change is what appears indubitably to be a decline of class as a factor shaping political behavior. In Britain, the country in which class has been outstandingly important, the behavioral indexes of this decline are striking. In Germany there are indications, such as the growing independence of voters, that suggest a similar trend. In France, as Berger shows, class is of little significance as a basis of party allegiance. The reasons for this decline inhere in modernization and can be found generally in advanced countries. Affluence, bureaucratization, and corporatist representation all play their familiar parts. Moreover, the rational, pragmatic, calculating spirit undermines not only sentiments of deference and noblesse oblige but also old solidarities of class identification. Sometimes the decline of class has been gradual, as in recent years; at other times it has been abrupt, as when the Nazi revolution, as Goldman shows, destroyed the powerful Junker class with its filiations in army and bureaucracy. In the long run, despite some powerful countercurrents, modernization in the past two or three centuries has deeply eroded the class distinctions inherited from the awesome inequalities of medievalism.

It may seem curious to speak of the decline of class in view of the role that class-based economic organizations have played in recent years in making difficult the attempts of Western governments to manage and control their economies. A principal problem has been the difficulty of coping with inflationary pressures. In particular, attempts at more programmatic planning, as by the Labour government of Harold Wilson, have foundered on the problem of controlling the wage-push elements of inflation. But even in *étatist* France governments have been unable to effectuate an incomes policy. As Berger observes, planning was forced by the wage-price problem to recede from its more ambitious efforts. Although Germany with its "social-market" economy has not attempted control on so wide a scale as France and Britain, the government of Willy Brandt has found its ambitious social program frustrated by the compulsions of an inflationary economy. Both social-democratic Sweden and free-enterprise America have been confronted by a wage-push inflation that has proved intractable.

It is not an adequate analysis to blame these trends on the "monopoly power" of labor organizations. We must note that the same basic problem afflicts countries with strong and with weak labor organizations. A more fundamental condition than monopoly power is almost the very opposite —that is, the absence of strong authority in the trade-union sector. Effective control of the economy, whether we call it planning or not, requires organization of the various sectors, on the side of both management and labor, in such a form that firm and binding agreements can be made between the planning government and the agents of production. This necessity has been a principal cause of the rise of corporatism in the present stage of modernization.

Oligopoly in business facilitates such negotiations and agreements, but the organization of business is often incommensurate with the needs. On the labor side, the problem is still more acute. Even where the top trade-union leadership is aware of the necessities of economic control, as they often are, they have been losing the capacity to bring along their rank and file. As a result the wildcat strike has become typical, tending to displace the old-fashioned official, nationwide strike. Governments cannot plan because labor itself has been losing its behavioral coherence. Entirely in contrast to the situation in the 1930s, it is not a polarization of classes that constitutes the problem, but rather a fragmentation of classes.

Generally, a politics of fragmentation characterizes the new trends of the present phase of modernity. This new politics rejects the corporatistic structures of economic planning and management. It emphasizes ad hoc voluntary associations, in contrast to permanent, class-based parties. In its eyes, participation in decision making becomes almost as important as the content and effect of the decisions themselves. Partly for this reason, centralization is shunned and local and regional forms preferred. One powerful current is represented by the revival of old nationalisms, as in Celtic Britain or Breton France. Sometimes it seems as if the energies withdrawn from the old solidarities of class are being projected upon the even older solidarities of regional nationality and that a communal politics might displace the class politics that has reigned so long.

Some observers see precisely such a future for European politics as communal loyalties flourish, nationality declines, and, they hope, European integration creates a wider polity. There is good reason to connect the rise of communal loyalties with the decline of nationality and to find a reason for the fragmentation of politics and the weakening of national authority in the changing function of the nation-state abroad. In this respect there are again parallels between the experiences of Russia and the democratic countries. With regard to Russia, Ulam attaches great importance to this connection, which he examines in some detail. The rise of dissent in recent years reflects some loss of authority as compared with the old days of high-pressure industrialization and Stalinist terror. While such dissent is neither organized, widespread, nor fundamental, Ulam does see some possibility that a "drastic change" might arise from developments in the international situation, specifically within international communism. The internal authority of the regime and its Communist elite has depended heavily upon the leadership by the Soviet Union of a unified, world-wide movement that promised to go on from strength to strength. The failure of communism to progress and, more important, the divisions within the movement and the assertion of a rival leadership by Communist China have weakened the hold of the authoritarian regime upon the loyalty and support of the Russian people. Ulam speculates that disillusionment with the regime and internal pressures for its liberalization could ultimately reach the point of undermining its ideological and organizational foundations.

Over the past generation the nations of Western Europe have suffered a not entirely dissimilar eclipse. Their role in the world has been reduced by the loss of empire, as in the case of Britain, France, Holland, and Belgium, and by the loss of influence in the face of the two superpowers, Russia and the United States. More recently and more importantly, the state apparatus of these nations has appeared to be less and less important not merely as an instrument of imperialism and influence but as an instrument of defense. The détente that developed between Russia and the United States in the sixties, dating especially from the nuclear test ban of 1963, has reduced the widespread fears of the Cold War period, as can readily be seen in the decline in defense budgets. In the West European countries, as in Russia, it is reasonable to suppose that a loss of external function has promoted a loss of internal authority. This decline in national authority gives the old communal loyalties the opportunity to assert their centrifugal claims.

Major problems of the advanced polities of the present day derive from fundamental traits of political modernity. To be sure, as other forces have shaped these political systems, so also problems can be found that derive from sources extraneous to modernity and modernization. The old and acute problem of liberty in Russia, for example, has such roots, and the tensions it creates cannot be explained merely by reference to the forces of modernization. Yet while modernization does not and should not pretend to explain everything about the polities we call modern, it does serve to bring out traits, trends, and problems of fundamental importance. At certain times in the past, such as the 1930s, the ideas of capitalism and capitalist development have similarly served to light up the nature of many contemporary problems. Today modernization theory performs this function of helping us understand the polities in which we live and which we may seek to preserve, change, or supersede.

Statistical Appendixes

Appendix A. A Comparison of the United States, the United Kingdom, France, Germany, and the Soviet Union

	Year	United States	United Kingdom	France	Germany	Soviet Union
I. Population						
(in Thousands)	1970	203,184	55,534	50,320	58,707	241,748
Population Growth (Average Annual Percent)	1963–1969	1.2	0.6	0.9	0.9	1.1
II. Area (in Thousands of Square Miles)		3,675	94	210	96	8,599
Population Density (Inhabitants Per Square Mile)	1970	57	593	239	602	29
III. Urbanization[1]						
Population in Metropolitan Areas Over 100,000 (in Percent)	1969	55.5	53.3	31.4	32.8	25.2
IV. Industrialization						
Civilian Labor Force by Main Sectors of Economic Activity (in Percent)	1969					
Agriculture		4.5	2.9	14.7	9.5	29.0
Industry		32.6	45.9	39.9	48.8	36.0
Services		59.4	49.1	44.0	41.1	35.0
V. National Accounts						
Gross National Product						
(in Billions of U.S. Dollars)	1969	947.8	109.8	140.0	152.9	358.0[2]
G.N.P. Per Capita (in U.S. Dollars)	1969	4,664	1,976	2,783	2,512	1,520[2]
Breakdown of G.N.P.	1969					
Private and Government Consumption (in Percent)		82	81	74	71	72
Capital Formation (in Percent)		18	18	26	26	27
Public Services (as Percent of G.N.P.)						
General Government	1968	32.0	39.0	38.9	37.5	—
National Defense	1969	8.6	5.1	4.4	3.5	8.5[5]
Social Security Expenditure	1966	7.2	12.6	15.5	15.5	11.1
Education	1969	5.8	5.8	4.4	3.6	7.3

128

VI. Economic Growth						
Average Annual Rates of Growth in G.N.P., Market Prices						
1950–1960		2.9	2.7	4.4	7.7	10.4
1960–1968		5.1	3.0	5.6	4.5	7.1
Average Annual Rates of Growth in G.N.P., Constant Prices						
1959–1969		4.3	3.0	5.9	5.1	—
Per Capita		2.9	2.3	4.8	4.0	5.8
VII. Education						
Numbers Attending School and University Full-time (in Thousands)	1967	55,070	10,098	11,205	10,506	61,344
Total Population (in Percent)		28.4	18.2	19.6	14.4	26.1
Numbers in Higher Education (in Thousands)	1967	6,085	267	509	219	4,123
VIII. Health						
Population Per Hospital Bed	1968	120	100	150	80	107
Population Per Physician	1968	650	860	770	620	433
IX. Material Indexes (U.S. = 100) (Per Capita)						
Energy Consumption	1968	100	50	38	44	39
Steel Production	1968	100	62	53	86	63
Motor Vehicles	1968	100	49	54	51	1.4
Newspapers	1968	100	160	80	108	105
Television Sets	1968	100	71	50	66	32

[1] Based on national calculations furnished by the United Nations. German and Soviet data include only cities, not their metropolitan areas.
[2] 1967 Estimate; Institute of Strategic Studies.
[3] Based on estimates; actual union membership statistics are unreliable.
[4] No data reported for 1968.
[5] This figure is certainly too low, since in Russia some defense expenditure is listed under civilian industry.

DATA SOURCES: United Nations, *Statistical Yearbook, 1970;* United Nations, *Yearbook of National Accounts Statistics, 1970;* United Nations, *Compendium of Social Statistics, 1968;* International Labour Office, *Yearbook of Labour Statistics, 1970;* Statistical Office of the European Communities, *Basic Statistics of the Community, 1970;* United States, Department of Commerce, *Statistical Abstract of the United States, 1971;* United Kingdom, Central Statistical Office, *Annual Abstract of Statistics, 1970;* France, *Annuaire Statistique de la France, 1969;* Germany, *Statistisches Jahrbuch für die Bundesrepublik Deutschland, 1970;* Institute of Strategic Studies, *The Strategic Balance, 1969–1970.*

The Statistical Appendixes were prepared by Glenn A. Robinson.

Appendix A (*continued*)

	Year	United States	United Kingdom	France	Germany	Soviet Union
X. Labor Statistics						
Working Population (in Thousands)	1969	69,877	25,825	20,439	26,342	99,130
Salaried Employees (as Percent of Working Population)	1969	82.8	89.4	74.4	81.0	66.4
Self-Employed (as Percent of Working Population)	1969	11.3	6.8	17.0	11.2	2.7
Unemployment, Average Rate	1961–1969	4.7	1.8	1.4	1.0	—
Trade Union Membership (in Thousands)	1967	19,181	9,970	3,880[3]	6,482	80,000
Industrial Disputes: Average Working Days Lost Annually Per 1,000 Workers in Mining, Manufacturing, Construction, Transport	1960–1969	1010	272	262[4]	22	—
Hourly Wage, Average in Nonagricultural Sectors (in U.S. Dollars)	1970	3.21	1.29	.84	1.66	—
Labor Productivity, Growth (1960 = 100)	1969	130	111	159	152	—
XI. Breakdown of Government Expenditures and Revenues (All Levels of Government)	1969					
Expenditures (in Percent)						
National Defense		24.1	11.7	11.8	9.5	12.4[5]
External Relations		1.1	1.5	1.0	0.3	—
Highways, Transport, Commerce		7.6	7.3	4.2	7.2	
Industry and Trade		1.3	9.4	7.4	6.9	43.0
Agriculture, Natural Resources		2.7	2.7	4.0	4.5	
Housing		0.6	5.7	2.7	4.2	—
Education		20.6	11.8	11.9	7.6	16.9
Social Welfare		26.2	19.7	24.9	34.0	14.6
Health		6.2	11.6	12.8	15.7	6.4
Debt Interest		6.8	10.2	5.6	6.8	—
Other		2.8	8.4	13.7	3.3	6.7
		100.0	100.0	100.0	100.0	100.0

Revenues (in Percent)						
Direct Taxes on Households		36.2	28.5	12.5	22.3	8.8
Social Security Contributions		17.8	13.5	38.4	28.4	—
Direct Taxes on Corporations		15.6	6.6	4.9	6.1	—
Indirect Taxes		30.2	43.5	42.0	36.8	32.2
Income from Public Enterprise		—	7.5	1.6	5.1	34.8
Other		0.2	0.4	0.6	1.3	24.2
		100.0	100.0	100.0	100.0	100.0
XII. Public Expenditure						
Total Public Expenditure	1969					
(Billions of U.S. Dollars)		334.8	47.4	40.9	64.3	—
(as Percent of G.N.P.)		35.3	43.2	40.3	42.1	—
Defense Expenditure per Capita (in U.S. Dollars)	1969	393	100	123	116	164[5]
Social Security Benefits Per Capita (in U.S. Dollars)	1966	260	228	321	334	238
XIII. Degree of Centralization						
Central Government Expenditures, Current Account (as Percent of Government Expenditures)	1969	54.0	73.0	55.1	35.8	—
Employees at Different Levels of Government (in Percent)	1967					
National		24.2	42.3	59.3	9.4	—
State		21.8	—	—	54.4	—
Local		54.0	57.7	40.7	36.2	—
XIV. Government Employees (as Percent of Working Population)	1967	17.7	5.8	7.2	11.1	18.3
XV. Annual Rates of Growth in Government Expenditures, Market Prices						
1950–1960		3.2	0.7	2.5	4.9	—
1960–1968		5.7	2.6	3.3	4.4	—

[1] Based on national calculations furnished by the United Nations. German and Soviet data include only cities, not their metropolitan areas.
[2] 1967 Estimate; Institute of Strategic Studies.
[3] Based on estimates; actual union membership statistics are unreliable.
[4] No data reported for 1968.
[5] This figure is certainly too low, since in Russia some defense expenditure is listed under civilian industry.

131

Appendix B. Growth of the Electorates: Great Britain, France, and Germany, 1870–1970

	Great Britain				France				Germany		
Year	Registered Electorate (in Thousands)	% of Population in Electorate	% Voting in Election	Year	Registered Electorate (in Thousands)	% of Population in Electorate	% Voting in Election	Year	Registered Electorate (in Thousands)	% of Population in Electorate	% Voting in Election
1832	813	3.3									
1868	2,298	7.5						1871	7,975	19.5	50.7
1874	2,810	8.6		1877	9,948	25.6	80.8				
1880	3,032	8.8		1881	10,124	27.2	68.5	1881	9,090	20.0	56.1
1886	5,734	15.8		1886	10,181	26.2	77.5				
1895	6,412	16.4		1893	10,443	27.2	71.5	1890	10,146	20.6	71.2
1900	6,731	16.4	74.6	1902	10,863	27.9	77.6	1903	12,531	21.4	75.8
1906	7,264	16.8	82.6								
1910	7,694	17.0	86.6	1910	11,327	28.8	77.3	1912	14,441	21.8	84.5
1918	21,392	45.6	58.9	1919	11,436	29.2	71.3	1919	36,766	59.4	82.6
1924	21,731	48.5	76.3	1924	11,070	27.7	83.0	1924	38,987	61.5	76.3
1929	28,850	62.4	76.1	1928	11,396	28.0	83.8	1928	41,224	63.4	74.6
1931	29,960	65.0	76.7	1932	11,741	28.2	83.5	1932	44,227	67.8	83.4
1935	31,379	67.8	71.2	1936	11,768	28.1	84.2				
1945	33,240	67.8	72.7	1945	24,623	61.4	79.1				
1950	33,269	66.7	84.0	1951	24,531	58.1	80.2	1949	31,207	63.5	78.5
1955	34,858	68.5	76.7	1956	26,775	61.2	82.8	1953	33,121	64.8	86.0
1959	35,397	68.1	78.8	1958	27,736	62.1	77.1	1957	35,401	66.0	87.8
1964	35,892	66.4	77.1	1962	27,535	59.5	68.7	1961	37,441	66.8	87.7
1966	35,965	65.6	75.8	1967	28,291	57.5	80.9	1965	38,510	65.0	86.8
1970	39,384	70.9	72.0	1968	28,171	56.7	80.1	1969	38,677	63.8	86.7

DATA SOURCES: *Annuaire statistique de la France, 1969*; *L'Année Politique*; David Butler and Jennie Freeman, *British Political Facts, 1900–1968* (London: 1969); Peter Campbell, *French Electoral Systems and Elections Since 1789* (Hamden: 1958); *Dod's Parliamentary Companion* 1843, 1852, 1874, 1880, 1886, 1895; François Goguel and Alfred Grosser, *La Politique en France* (Paris: 1964); Georges LaChapelle, *Les Élections Législatives: Résultats Officiels* (Paris:1914, 1919, 1928, 1932, 1936); Frederick H. McCalmont, *The Parliamentary Poll Book of All Elections 1832–1895* (London:1895); *Statistisches Jahrbuch für das deutsche Reich, 1933*; *Statistisches Jahrbuch für die Bundesrepublik Deutschland, 1970*; Walter Tormin, *Geschichte der deutschen Parteien seit 1848* (Stuttgart: 1964).

Select Bibliography

General Theory

Almond, Gabriel, and G. Bingham Powell. *Comparative Politics: A Developmental Approach.* Boston: Little, Brown, 1966.

Deutsch, Karl. *The Nerves of Government: Models of Political Communication and Control.* Glencoe, Ill.: Free Press, 1963.

Easton, David. *A Systems Analysis of Political Life.* New York: Wiley, 1965.

Friedrich, Carl J. *Man and His Government: An Empirical Theory of Politics.* 2 vols. New York: McGraw-Hill, 1963.

Macridis, Roy O. *The Study of Comparative Government.* New York: Doubleday, 1955.

Merriam, Charles E. *Systematic Politics.* Chicago: University of Chicago Press, 1946.

Parsons, Talcott. *The Social System.* Glencoe, Ill.: Free Press, 1951.

Richter, Melvin (ed.). *Essays in Theory and History: An Approach to the Social Sciences.* Cambridge, Mass.: Harvard University Press, 1970.

Shils, Edward (ed.). *Toward a General Theory of Social Action.* Cambridge, Mass.: Harvard University Press, 1951.

Weber, Max. *Theory of Social and Economic Organization.* A. M. Henderson and Talcott Parsons (trs.). New York: Oxford University Press, 1947.

Modernization and Development

Apter, David. *The Politics of Modernization.* Chicago: University of Chicago Press, 1965.

Black, C. E. *The Dynamics of Modernization.* New York: Harper & Row, 1966.

Durkheim, Emile. *The Division of Labor in Society.* George Simpson (tr.). New York: Free Press, 1933.

Greer, Scott. *The Emerging City: Myth and Reality.* Glencoe, Ill.: Free Press, 1962.

Huntington, Samuel P. *Political Order in Changing Societies.* New Haven, Conn. and London: Yale University Press, 1968.

Lerner, Daniel, et al. *The Passing of Traditional Society: Modernizing the Middle East.* Glencoe, Ill.: Free Press, 1958.

Mannheim, Karl. *Man and Society in an Age of Reconstruction.* New York: Harcourt, Brace, 1940.

Moore, Barrington. *Social Origins of Dictatorship and Democracy.* Boston: Beacon Press, 1969.

Organski, F. K. *The Stages of Political Development.* New York: Knopf, 1965.

Rostow, W. W. *Politics and the Stages of Growth.* Cambridge, England: Cambridge University Press, 1971.

Rustow, Dankwart. *A World of Nations: The Problems of Political Modernization.* Washington, D.C.: Brookings Institution, 1967.

Tilly, Charles (ed.). *The Building of States in Western Europe.* Forthcoming.

Wilson, Godfrey, and Monica Wilson. *The Analysis of Social Change.* Cambridge, England: Cambridge University Press, 1945.

Index

Almond, Gabriel, 26n
The Analysis of Social Change (Wilson and Wilson), 70
Aquinas, Thomas, 61
Aristocracy, as stage in political development, 98
Austria, idea of sovereignty in, 84
Authority
  concepts of, 41
  and law, 63
  in Russia, 115–118
  problems of, in modernity, 119–125

Bacon, Francis, 62
Bagehot, Walter, 25, 43–44, 60
Behaviorism, in political science, 25
Belief systems
  defined, 27–29
  vs. value systems, 30–31
Bentley, Arthur F., 25n
Bevan, Aneurin, 38
Bias, ideological, sources of, 32
Bismarck, Otto von, 116
Black, Cyril E., 62n
Bodin, Jean, concept of sovereignty, 82–83
Bourbon monarchy, 96
  legal theory, 84
  power structure, 85
  achievements, 99–100
  see also France; French Revolution
Brademas, Hon. John, 76n
Brandt, Willy, 123

Bryce, James, 25
Bureaucracy, 43
  and patterns of power, 50–51, 52
  increase in scale of, 73, 74
  and sovereignty, 82–84
  historical development, 84–86
  and effectiveness, 113–114
  Russian, 113–114
Burke, Edmund, 66, 87
  on expressive symbolism, 38–39

Capitalism
  and secularism, 88
  dependence on state action, 101
Centralization
  result of output expansion, 79
  measurement of, 79
  in Great Britain, 102–103
  in Russia, 113–114
Citizen, and pattern of power, 50–51
Class
  and political systems, 20–21
  conflict, and modernity, 93
  and collectivist stage of development, 110–111
  economic, and authority, 120–121
  decline as influence in politics, 122–123
Cognitive map, 31, 36
  defined, 26
  and belief system, 27
  and response, 29
Coke, Sir Edward, on sovereign power, 83–84
Colbert, Jean Baptiste, 85

135

Collectivism
    and patterns of interest, 49
    of policy, 53
    early appearance in modernity, 88–89
    emergence in Great Britain, 95
    as stage in political development, 108–111
    and authority, 121
Common Market, 69
Communism, moral basis of, 31
Constitution (U.S.), 63
Cultural-structural model, elements of, 46–57, 94
Culture. See Political culture
Cumulation and development, 97–98
Cunningham, William, 98n

De Gaulle, Charles, 115
Demand-creation, role of intellectuals in, 66
Democracy in America (Tocqueville), 25
Democratization
    as expression of voluntarism, 64
    and expanding expectations, 65
    as stage of political development, 102–108
Development
    history as, 59–60
    by stages, 94–98
Dewey, John, means-ends-consequences model, 15–17
The Division of Labor in Society (Durkheim), 70
Domination
    Weber's concept of, 18–19
    legitimate, vs. mutual adjustment, 76
Durkheim, Emile, 67
    on specialization, 70

Economic events, and political systems, 3–4
Economy
    interaction with polity, 56–57
    in pattern of power, 57
    segmented vs. developed, 72
    vs. state, 76
    and decline of class, 122–123
Edict of Nantes (1598), 87
Effectiveness, as problem of modern polity, 113–118
Electorates, growth, 1870–1970, 132
The Emerging City: Myth and Reality (Greer), 70
Emerson, Rupert, on the nation, 35
Engels, Friedrich, on class and state, 12
England. See Great Britain
Environment and economy, 56–57
Equality and class conflict, 93
Etzioni, Amitai, 92n
European Common Market, 69
Expressive symbolism
    effect on political culture, 34–35
    and nationality, 35
    elements of, 36–37
    functions, 37–38

The Federalist, 12, 48
Finer, Herman, on Prussian bureaucratic monarchy, 85–86
Fox, William T. R., 92
Fragmentation, politics of, 121–125
France
    idea of sovereignty in, 84
    bureaucracy, 85
    Edict of Nantes (1598), 87
    secularism, 87
    nationalism, 91
    development of liberal democracy, 104–105
    collectivist stage of development, 110–111
    democratic pluralism, 115
    class interests, 122
    compared with U.S., Great Britain, Germany, and Russia, 128–131
    growth of electorate, 132
    see also Bourbon monarchy; French Revolution

Frederick William the Great, Elector of Brandenburg, 84, 86
French Revolution, 99, 100, 107
and British economy, 70
effects, 95, 96
and modern values, 95, 96–97, 104
Freud, Sigmund, 38

Galbraith, John Kenneth, 69
Germany
constitution, 42
nationalism in, 91, 100
modernization and Nazi revolution, 95–96
absolutism and modernization, 100–101
liberal democracy in, 105–106
class and Nazi revolution, 122
compared with Great Britain, U.S., France, and Russia, 128–131
growth of electorate, 132
see also Prussia; Weimar Republic
Great Britain
House of Commons and expressive symbolism, 37–38
effects of French Revolution in, 70
idea of sovereignty in, 83–84
bureaucracy in, 86
secularism, 87
Toleration Act (1689), 87
economic collectivism, 89
nationalism, 91
lulls in political conflict, 95
Puritan revolution, 95
aristocratic stage of development, 98–99
development of liberal democracy, 102–104
growth of government expenditure, 103
collectivist stage of development, 108–109
class interests, 110, 120–121, 122
democratic pluralism, 115

compared with U.S., France, Germany, and Russia, 128–131
growth of electorate, 132
Greer, Scott, 70

Hallowell, John H., on politics as purposive action, 47–48
Henderson, A. M., 18n
Henry VIII (England), 28
Herring, E. P., on democracy and control, 53
Herrschaft (domination), Max Weber's concept of, 18–19
History, and political science, 58–60
Hobbes, Thomas, on sovereignty, 83
Hume, David, 40

Identification
and expressive symbolism, 38
psychological roots, 40
Ideology
Marxism-Leninism as, 31
sources of bias, 31–34
role in legitimacy, 119–120
Incoherence, as result of democratic pluralism, 114–115, 118
Induction theory, problems of, 32–33
Industrialization
impact on polity, 55–56
and division of labor, 68–69, 71
Inflation, wage-push, 122–123
An Inquiry into the Nature and Causes of the Wealth of Nations (Smith), 68
Institutes of the Laws of England (Coke), 83–84
Intellectuals, role in demand-creation, 66
Interdependence
and increase in specialization and scale, 71–73
networks, in nation building, 77
as result of government action, 78–79
Interest, patterns of
defined, 22

Interest, patterns of (*continued*)
  and legitimacy, 43
  elements of, 47–50
  mobilization of, 55–56
  and patterns of power, 74–76
  sovereignty in, 86

Jennings, Ivor, 43

Labor, division of
  as concept of economic analysis, 68–69
  see also Specialization
Laissez faire, 103, 113
Language, as symbolic behavior, 26–27
Law, and authority, 63
Lefebvre, Georges, on French national integration, 100
Legitimacy, 21, 22, 76
  and modernization, 5, 119
  and *Herrschaft,* 18–20
  and political culture, 23
  conceptions of, 39–45
  and effect on political domination, 77
  role of ideology in, 119–120
Legitimists (Bourbon), 41
Leviathan (Hobbes), 83
Liberalism, as element of modernity, 89–90
Liberty
  and modernity, 89–90
  as Whig ideal, 98
Lindblom, Charles E., 76n
Lipson, E., 89n
Locke, John, 66, 87
  political system model, 11–12
Louis XIV (France), 84, 85
Lysenkoism, 118

Magna Carta Libertatum, 89
Malraux, André, on nation and social justice, 77–78
Managerialism, as new elitism, 49
Mannheim, Karl, 32
Marshall, Alfred, 68–69, 71

Marshall, T. H., 97
Marx, Karl, 66
Marxism, political systems model of, 12
Marxism-Leninism, as ideology, 31
McIlwain, Charles H., 83
Means-end continuum model
  as defined by John Dewey, 15–17
  and *Herrschaft,* 18–19
  and class, 20
  and purposive action, 21–22
Middle Ages, 67
  teleological conception of authority, 63, 64
  absence of sovereignty concept, 82, 83
  and nationality, 90–91
Models
  components of, 10–11
  types, 11–13
  uses, 12, 14
  as not value-free, 14
  means-end-consequences continuum, 15–17
  cultural-structural, 46–57, 94
Modernity
  and loss of purpose, 4–5
  and dominance of technique, 6–7
  response to problems, 7–8
  and capitalism, 88
  and nationality, 90
  and human purpose, 93
  and class conflict, 93
  authority problems in, 119–125
Modernization
  effect on purpose, 5
  and science, 6–7
  theory of, and understanding political systems, 7–8, 112
  and industrialization, 55–56
  as historical development, 58–60
  scientific rationalism in, 61–62
  and voluntarism, 62–64
  and conceptions of authority, 63, 119
  and democratization, 64–65
  economic, 66–73

political, 73–78
secularism in, 87–88
aristocratic stage, 98–101
liberal democratic stage, 102–108
collectivist stage, 108–111
as source of pluralism, 115
Montesquieu, Baron de, 25, 84n, 98
Moynihan, Daniel Patrick, 55n, 75
Myrdal, Gunnar, 121
on national integration, 77

Napoleon I, 100, 105
Nation
state building of, 76–78
development of, 92–93
Nationalism
and conceptions of legitimacy, 78
defined, 90
origins, 90–91
development, 92–93
as source of authority, 120
as revived of old, 123
Nationality
as expressive action, 35–36
and modernity, 90
Neumann, Franz, on monarchy, 84
Neumann, Sigmund, 47n
The New Industrial State (Galbraith), 69
Nietzsche, Friedrich, 66
Normative map, 31, 36
defined, 26
and response, 30

The Old Regime and the Revolution (Tocqueville), 85
Origin of the Family, Private Property and the State (Engels), 12
Osgood, Charles E., 24n
Output
as exercise of state's power, 79
expansion of, as centralization, 79
budgeting, 80

Parsons, Talcott, 18n, 27, 36
concept of political culture, 25–26

concept of expressive symbolism, 34
Patriotism, and stability, 92
Patterns of power
defined, 22
elements of, 50–52
mobilization of, 56
economy in, 57
and pattern of interest, 74–76
and bureaucracy, 86
see also Power
Peacock, Alan T., 103
Peter the Great, 87, 96, 107
Pluralism, as problem of modernization, 115–116, 117–118
Policy, patterns of
defined, 22
elements of, 52–55
Political culture
patterns of, 23
defined, 25
and political orientation, 26
as product of symbolic behavior, 26–27
as coordinator of political action, 28–29
as source of conflict, 43–44
Political order, problem of, 18–22
Political systems
and economic events, 3–4
problems of analysis, 10
classical models of, 11–14
means-end-consequences continuum model of, 15–17
essential components, 18
and class, 20–21
and history, 58–59
Politics
and class, 20–21
and vision, 21–22
of fragmentation, 121–125
Power
mobilization of, 56, 73–74
measurement of, 80
see also Patterns of power
Principles of Economics (Marshall), 68

Prussia
    idea of sovereignty in, 84
    bureaucracy in, 85–86, 96
    modernization in, 100–101, 105
    see also Germany
Puritanism, affected by modernity, 5
Purpose
    loss of, defined, 4–5
    effect of modernization on, 6–7
    and means-end-consequences model, 21–22
    relationship to legitimacy, 41–43
    as element in struggle for power, 47–48
    forms of, 60–61
    and rationalism, 62

Rabelais, François, 63
Rationalism, scientific, 61–62
    forms, 61
    as element of modernity, 63–64, 101
    as source of bureaucracy, 82
Reflections on the Revolution in France (Burke), 38
Reformism, as policy objective, 86–87
Renan, Ernest, 92, 93
    on nationality, 35
Revolution
    and political development, 95–97
    see also French Revolution
Richelieu, Armand Jean de Plessis, Cardinal, Duke of, 85
Robespierre, Maximilien, 105
Rousseau, Jean Jacques, 18, 44, 66, 83
    political systems model, 12–13
Russia
    sovereignty in, 84
    secularism in, 87–88
    nationalism, 91, 92
    effects of Revolution in, 95, 96
    18th century modernization, 101
    absence of liberalism in, 106–108
    collectivism, 110
    problems of bureaucracy, 113–114
    problems of authority, 115–118, 124
    compared with U.S., Great Britain, France, and Germany, 128–131

Saint-Just, Louis de, 105
Scale
    as process of economic development, 69–72
    applied to political development, 73, 74, 78
Schattschneider, E. E., functional concept of politics, 47–48
Schattschneider's law, 47, 48
Schumpeter, Joseph A., 99
    on group demands in political arena, 65
Science
    influence on modernization, 6–7
    and problem of inductive leap, 32–34
Second Treatise of Government (Locke), 11
Secularism
    and pattern of policy, 82
    historical emergence of, 87
Self-interest, as stability factor in politics, 40
Shelley, Percy Bysshe, 66
Six Books of the Commonwealth (Bodin), 82–83
Smith, Adam, 99, 109
    concept of division of labor, 68, 69–70
Social Contract (Rousseau), 13, 83
Sovereignty, theories of, 82–86
Specialization
    as economic concept, 69–72
    applied to political development, 74, 78
    see also Division of labor
Stalin, Joseph, 118
State
    as source of human values, 13
    nation building by, 76–78
    output as exercise of power of, 79

control and effectiveness, 113–114
  see also Welfare state
Symbolism. See Expressive symbolism

Taxation
  development in France, 99–100
  increases in, 121
Technique, dominance of, 6–7
Technocracy, as result of modernization, 75
Teleology vs. modernity, 63–64
Tilly, Charles, 88, 109
  on history as past behavior, 58
Tocqueville, Alexis de, 25, 85
Toleration Act (1689), 87
Toynbee, Arnold, 67
Tudor monarchs, and idea of sovereignty, 83

United Kingdom. See Great Britain
United States
  conception of authority in, 63
  technocracy in, 75–76
  compared with Great Britain, France, Germany, and Russia, 128–131

Value systems
  components, 29–30
  distinguished from belief systems, 30–31
Victorianism, affected by modernity, 5
Voluntarism
  defined, 62–63
  as element of modernity, 63–64
  and democracy, 64–65
  and concept of sovereignty, 82

Weber, Max, 20, 25, 85, 102
  concept of *Herrschaft*, 18–19
  on industrialization, 62
Weimar Republic, 106, 110
  and democratic pluralism, 114–115
Welfare state
  structures of interdependence in, 76–77
  rise of, 103–104, 109
  and authority, 122
Wellington, Duke of, 105
What Is a Nation? (Renan), 92
Whitehead, Alfred North, 33
Wilson, Godfrey, 70
Wilson, Harold, 123
Wilson, Monica, 70
Winstanley, Gerrard, 89
Wiseman, Jack, 103

About the Author

Samuel H. Beer, general editor of *Patterns of Government* and author of Part 1, "Modern Political Development," and Part 2, "The British Political System," is Eaton Professor of the Science of Government at Harvard University. He studied at the University of Michigan and Oxford University and won his Ph.D. at Harvard. Chairman of the Department of Government at Harvard from 1954 to 1958, he is the author of *The City of Reason, Treasury Control,* and *British Politics in the Collectivist Age,* which was given the Woodrow Wilson Award as the "best book on politics, government or international affairs published in the United States in 1965." He served as Vice-President of the American Political Science Association in 1964–1965, has held Fulbright and Guggenheim Fellowships, and was Messenger Lecturer at Cornell University in 1969. His principal fields of interest are comparative politics and American federalism, and he has published articles on political parties, economic planning, the British Parliament, the methodology of social science, state government, and American political thought. He has been active in Democratic party politics and recently served as a member of the McGovern-Fraser Commission on Delegate Selection and Party Structure.

JF
31
B415
1974

WITHDRAWN
From Library Collection

DATE DUE

MR 28			